PASSIONS AND INTERESTS

American Political Thought

edited by

Wilson Carey McWilliams and Lance Banning

PASSIONS AND INTERESTS

POLITICAL PARTY CONCEPTS OF AMERICAN DEMOCRACY

Gerald M. Pomper

University Press of Kansas

© 1992 by the University Press of Kansas

All rights reserved

Published by the University Press of Kansas (Lawrence, Kansas 66049), which was organized by the Kansas Board of Regents and is operated and funded by Emporia State University, Fort Hays State University, Kansas State University, Pittsburg State University, the University of Kansas, and Wichita State University

Library of Congress Cataloging-in-Publication Data

Pomper, Gerald M.
Passions and interests: political party concepts of American democracy / Gerald M. Pomper.
p.   cm. — (American political thought)
Includes index.
ISBN 0-7006-0551-7 (alk. paper) — ISBN 0-7006-0552-5 (pbk.)
1. Political parties—United States. 2. Democracy—United States.
I. Title. II. Series.
JK2261.P674   1992
324.273—dc20   92-12328

British Library Cataloguing in Publication Data is available.

Printed in the United States of America
10 9 8 7 6 5 4 3 2 1

CONTENTS

TABLES AND FIGURES

PREFACE

Political parties and democracy comprise the interwoven strands of this book. Their coupling exists on three levels: personal, empirical, and theoretical.

Least important to the reader is the personal connection, but it does exist. Political parties and democracy have stirred both my intellectual interests and my emotional passions since I first became aware of the larger world of politics. Tammany Hall bordered my New York elementary school, which also served as the local voting precinct. The connection between political parties and democracy was overtly physical to me, even before it became theoretical.

On the empirical level, history and political science draw a more scientific connection. From James Madison's creation of the first popular-based political party to yesterday's newspaper, we see the relationship. The growth of political parties and the extension of democracy proceed along parallel tracks. Competitive political parties facilitate, although they do not guarantee, a considerable measure of popular involvement, control, and policy determination. Without them, government is more likely to evidence authoritarianism, violence, and repression. Rajiv Gandhi once said that India's greatest political need was a strong opposition party; his subsequent assassination underlined the point in blood.

Most important is the theoretical connection, and this book is intended to bridge two areas within the discipline of political science: the study of political philosophy and the study of parties. Perhaps that bridge cannot be built or is poorly constructed here, and I will only cause dissatisfaction among two diverse groups of academic specialists. But I hope that the ideas here will be useful for both theorists and empiricists.

Exploring the relationship between political parties and democracy can enrich each of these subjects. Such a relationship has been the focus of some of the most insightful works in political science, beginning with the classic books of Michels and Ostrogorski, but it has been neglected for most of the second half of the twentieth century. Alan Ware suggests some explanations for the decline: "There was a fragmenting of research from about the 1950s onwards, so that those scholars who were concerned with the nature of the concept of democracy . . . were no longer the same people who had great expertise in the working of political institutions. Moreover, interest in the empirical study of politics moved sharply away from institutions like parties to focus on other aspects of the political process."[1]

As the troubled twentieth century nears its end, democracy and competitive parties are receiving renewed attention, and I believe this is an appropriate time to again consider their relationship. This volume is my contribution to that major task.

In writing this book, I have received much help. I am particularly indebted intellectually to two colleagues: Wilson Carey McWilliams has continued to teach me about politics and political theory; and Carolyn Nestor has been an insightful and diligent research assistant. My work has been greatly improved by volunteers reading chapter drafts, particularly Diana Owen as well as Debra Dodson, John Hart, Kenneth Janda, John Kessel, Maureen Moakley, Benjamin Radcliff, Gordon Schochet, and Patricia Sykes.

Over the years I have also gained much from the scholarship and personal support of M. J. Aronoff, Ross Baker, Vernon Bogdanor, Bill Crotty, Peter Gay, James Gibson, Stanley Kelley, Richard L. McCormick, Richard P. McCormick, Jerome Mileur, Austin Ranney, Alan Rosenthal, Stephen Salmore, Marian Simms, David Truman, and John White. The concepts in this book were first developed in my graduate teaching at Rutgers University. There, I learned as much as I taught, particularly from Joseph Cammarano, Kenneth Dautrich, John Dedrick, Patrick Deneen, Kim Downing, Stephen Dworetz, Cliff Fox, LeeAundra Preuss, Joseph Romance, Jens Runge, and Loretta Sernekos. I have previously published a version of chapter 1 in the *Journal of Theoretical Politics* and appreciate the courtesy of Sage Publications in allowing the material to be included in this book.

I completed this manuscript while enjoying a sabbatical semester at Australian National University, which provided a superb position as visiting professor and the efficient services of Thelma Williams and Joanna Phillips. I also appreciate the warm hospitality of new and old friends in Australia—Robert Dowse, Bruce Headey, Rick Kuhn, Elaine and Charles McCoy, and Bruce and Edna Smith.

As it has for decades, Rutgers University generously supported my research through an academic study leave and grants from its Research Council and Graduate School of Education. The Eagleton Institute of Politics has been a continuing source of personal and logistical help. Edith Saks, as always, merits particular thanks for her devotion and efficiency. Fred Woodward, director of the University Press of Kansas, provided regular encouragement, and Claire Sutton copy-edited the manuscript sympathetically.

Scholarship, like all of life, requires love to flourish. If there is merit in this work, it has been nourished most of all by three family generations: my parents, Moe and Celia Pomper, and my second parents, Emanuel and Lillian Michels; my wife, Marlene, and my brother, Isidor; my sons, David, Marc, and Miles, and my new daughters, Rayna and Erika. Their love, I confidently hope, will nurture our continuing family. I dedicate this book to the passions and interests of the next generation.

G.M.P.
Canberra, 1991

ONE
CONCEPTS OF POLITICAL PARTIES

After all these years, we do not know how democracy works.
—A Romanian protester, 1989[1]

From 1989 to 1991, the world was transformed by the political revolutions in Eastern Europe and the Soviet Union, the surge of democratic government in Latin America, and the repressed expression of popular protest in Beijing's Tiananmen Square. Central to these epochal events was a yearning for competitive political parties.

The rallying cry in these historic mass demonstrations, particularly in Eastern Europe, was neither Republican France's idealistic call for "liberty, equality, fraternity" nor Bolshevik Russia's substantive claim for "peace, bread, and land." Instead, there was a basic, if sometimes inchoate, understanding that freedom requires multiple political parties seeking power in fair and open elections. Soon after these historic events, the major nations of the world formally committed themselves to "the fundamental principles of multiparty democracy."[2] Empirical reality had validated E. E. Schattschneider's theoretical assertion "that the political parties created democracy and that modern democracy is unthinkable save in terms of the parties."[3]

In this book I accept, and explore, that premised relationship between political parties and democracy. My major task is to examine different conceptual models of political parties, primarily in the United States. In analyzing these concepts, I attempt to answer three questions: What are the meanings attributed to parties? Empirically, to what extent do American parties fit these conceptions? and How well do the different conceptions of parties serve democratic interests?

My focus is on theories of what parties can and should be rather than on theories of actual party behavior. Good theories surely should be tested against reality and appropriately revised to account for those realities. As I explore the different concepts of party, I attempt to match them to empirical research findings; these explorations may contribute to more general theories of parties and party systems.

My purpose, however, is not to construct an empirical theory of party behavior, because other scholars have significantly pursued that considerable task.[4] My aim here is more limited: to clarify and examine some important abstract concepts of parties. This work is important in itself. Ideas can have their own impact, leading to new interpretations of and even to changes in "the facts." We will understand parties better if we first understand their conceptual foundations.

In this chapter, I will explore these conceptual foundations and develop a framework for the theoretical and empirical analyses that follow. This initial material is admittedly abstract; a brief outline may help the reader follow my argument. In this chapter, I will

1. consider alternative definitions of political parties;
2. develop three analytic and dichotomous dimensions of parties, termed focus, goals, and modes;
3. combine these dimensions into eight ideal-type party concepts;
4. develop three analytic and dichotomous dimensions of democratic theory, congruent with the party dimensions, termed accessibility of leadership, goals, and participation;
5. speculate on the relationship between the party concepts and alternative political systems.

After readers have followed—or endured—this abstract argument, I will summarize the following chapters. These comprise substantive discussions of the party concepts and their relationship to democracy.

IDENTIFYING POLITICAL PARTIES

What is a political party? Academic convention requires that we begin with Edmund Burke's definition: "Party is a body of men united, for promoting by their joint endeavors the national interest, upon some particular principle in which they are all agreed."[5] Burke's criterion does present a normative standard for one kind of party; however, it is not a general definition of all parties but a particular defense of the Whig party of his day.

Burke presents a normative concept, what a party can or should be, in place of a descriptive definition, what parties are or do. The same difficulty exists in a major modern scholar's labors over etymology:

If it is wrong to neglect the association between part and party, it would also be quite wrong, on the other hand, to consider the party as a part that is unrelated to the whole. If a party is not a part capable of governing for the sake of the whole, that is, in view of a general interest, then it does not differ from a faction. Although a party only represents a part, this part must take a *non-partial* approach to the whole.[6]

James Madison was halfway closer to a useful definition when he characterized a faction (which in his time was not distinguished from a party) as "a number of citizens, whether amounting to a majority or minority of the whole, who are united and actuated by some common impulse of passion, or of interest, adverse to the rights of other citizens, or to the permanent and aggregate interests of the community."[7] As Albert Hirschman has shown, Madison expressed the philosophic effort of his era to employ interests to control passions.[8]

Apart from his normative criticism, Madison does provide a useful initial description of the meaning of party—a unified effort to affect government, deriving its force from group interests and popular passions. Parties may certainly be "adverse" to other groups, or they may govern in the general interest, as Sartori insists, but these effects must be determined by the parties' actions, not assumed in advance. In his life, rather than in his theory, Madison apparently accepted the distinction. Without apology for his party's passions and interests, he led in the creation of the first American political party, the Republicans who elected President Thomas Jefferson in 1800.

As Madison's career suggests, parties are a distinctive political group. As the combinations of interests and passions defined by Madison, parties are unique in that they are particularly oriented toward elections. Epstein includes this critical element in the most useful descriptive definition of parties: "any group, however loosely organized, seeking to elect governmental officeholders under a given label."[9]

Crucially, Epstein calls attention to the collective character of a political party, established by its common label, a characteristic that distinguishes parties from other power-seeking groups included in other formulations. These alternatives have defined a party as a group that "presents at elections, and is capable of placing through elections, candidates for public office"[10] or as an agency "for forging links between citizens and policymakers.''[11] Parties certainly want to place candidates in public office, but so do interest groups and financial contributors; although parties clearly promote linkage, so do individual candidates and opinion pollsters. Parties are unique in their nominal unity and in their electoral focus. This definition largely excludes from our consideration the ruling organizations in one-party states, such as the dominant Communist parties of the erstwhile Soviet bloc. Where a legitimate even if limited opposition exists, as in Mexico (or the old Democratic one-party South in the United States), the definition will still serve because elections remain important in legitimizing the dominant party's continuance in office.

Where party power cannot be challenged legitimately, elections become only a ritual. In these systems, parties obviously are important, indeed more important than their democratic counterparts, as agencies of government and social mobilization, but they are very different organizations. Although they still bear some family resemblance to democratic parties, they are too different to be considered even as part of the same genus.

A definition is not sufficient in itself but marks the beginning of fuller concepts that would delineate the expected organization, goals, and appeals of political parties. The most common conceptual framework in the study of political parties, derived from V. O. Key, distinguishes among "party as an organization," "party as an electorate," and "party in government."[12] This framework is certainly useful in describing the activities of parties; however, it incorrectly implies distinctions that are not empirically valid and neglects critical theoretical issues.

The United States does not have three different kinds of parties, each fitting a concept of a separate party engaged in organizing, electioneering, and governing. Instead, a large amount of mixing exists among these three presumably distinct entities. The "party as an organization" might be expected to choose its own leaders, but in reality they are selected, through primaries, by the voters, the "party as an electorate." Similarly, a large share of campaigning is done by officeholders, the "party in government," not by the formal organization. Nor is the party electorate a distinct group, for it is defined to a considerable extent by party organizational rules and statutes, such as registration, as well as by its responses to the actions of officeholders bearing the party label.

American parties are a jumble of these three conventional forms, which cannot readily be separated, as the presidential nomination illustrates. The nomination designates the choice of the party's leader, and it is formally determined in a convention of party activists. Yet, in reality, the choice is made primarily by the "party as an electorate," with some lesser influence by the "party as an organization" and the "party in government." The combination is formally acknowledged in the Democratic party, whose convention delegates include representatives of the organization (the Democratic National Committee), officeholders ("super-delegates"), and the electorate (primary election winners). Any concept of an American political party must recognize this blending.

Furthermore, the common tripartite division of political parties is conceptually defective. At best, it describes the separate activities of three kinds of people. A concept of a political party, however, must present some model of the party's total activities, of the intended if not actual interactions and linkages among organizers, voters, and governors. These linkages are particularly important in the study of democracy.

The tripartite framework impedes analysis of these vital democratic connections. As two critics argue, it gives attention only to "truncated" parties but "defines away the normative problem posed by traditional party thought," the proper relationship of leaders and led. Instead, the concept of party becomes an empty abstraction, "a superficial model ... in which the elite and mass distinction is erased."[13]

Useful concepts of political parties must emphasize, not neglect, how parties connect mass electorates with elite officials. For this purpose, it is best to distinguish parties, which are groups that contest elections, from the electorate itself. To capture the reality of party, as Schlesinger puts it, "We must exclude the voter. Voters are choosers among parties, not components of them."[14] In this book, I examine parties essentially as groups of people who seek power through the ballot box, not as voters who grant power through their ballots. Parties, then, are "working politicians *supported* by partisan voters."[15]

DIMENSIONS OF PARTY CONCEPTS

Concepts of political parties are more than descriptions of their activities; they are more comprehensive and deal more generally with normative expectations and empirical features. As conceptual models, furthermore, they are not intended simply to reflect reality but to illuminate and even change reality. In this book, I examine eight such concepts.

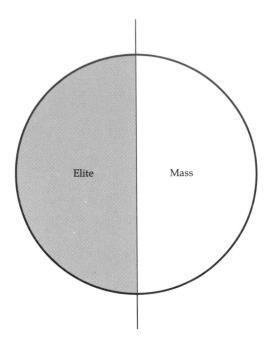

Figure 1.1. Concepts of Political Parties: Focus

The concepts applied to political parties can be classified by three analytic dimensions. First, concepts of parties differ in the breadth of their *focus*, dealing either with the active elite of the parties or with their larger mass clientele. Second, parties are seen as having different *goals*, stressing either collective or coalitional objectives. Third, concepts of parties differ in the understanding of the parties' *modes*, portraying them either as instrumental to other objectives or as directly expressive of affective sentiments.[16]

These are analytic dimensions, intended to describe ideal party types, not to predict their behavior. As polar opposites, these dichotomous categories allow us to probe more fully into the abstract concepts of parties. In reality, the divisions are not so neat and clear. An actual political party includes both elite and mass elements, pursues both collective and coalitional goals, and acts both instrumentally and expressively. Empirically, these dimensions differentiating party concepts are better represented as continua rather than as dichotomies, with any particular party emphasizing one or another side of each continuum.

Focus is the first dimension (see Figure 1.1).[17] Parties, by the definition

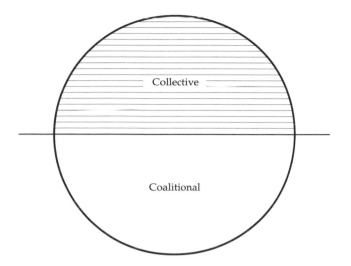

Figure 1.2. Concepts of Political Parties: Goals

used here, are always involved in contesting elections. This characteristic remains in both the elite and the mass foci, even when different aspects of the party are stressed. Illustratively, when we take an elite focus, we can examine the organizational bureaucracy of the party that prepares for these elections; when we take a mass focus, we can examine the party as a team of office seekers.

When alternative party concepts evidence a mass focus, they emphasize the parties' relationship to and activities in the larger political world. Attention centers on the party's relationships with important external audiences, including the media, financial contributors, and most important, the voters.[18] Political scientists' extensive studies of voting behavior examine the effect of these external activities, although they are not actual studies of parties.

A second dimension concerns the goals of parties (see Figure 1.2). We can assume that all parties have a general goal of winning elections. The more specific goals, however, can vary from collective to coalitional, e.g., from the achievement of a common policy program to the distribution of the spoils of office.

Collective goals are those that require united action for their achievement and, once achieved, provide benefits for the entire group, with only limited distribution to specific individuals. Concepts of political parties that focus on collective goals typically emphasize broad political programs and ideologies, dealing with public goods. Woodrow Wilson, himself a political scientist, provided a particularly eloquent expression of the collective purpose of a political party as he was inaugurated as president of the United States:

> No one can mistake the purpose for which the Nation now seeks to use the Democratic Party. It seeks to use it to interpret a change in its own plans and point of view. . . . Our duty is to cleanse, to reconsider, to restore, to correct the evil without impairing the good, to purify and humanize every aspect of our common life without weakening or sentimentalizing it.[19]

Coalition goals are more modest. They will also usually require concerted action for their achievement, but the achieved rewards typically will then be divided among the members of the coalition for their individual satisfaction. Public policies may constitute some of these rewards, not as a total and coherent ideological program but as a collection of particular programs benefiting distinct groups. An American party platform is illustrative, providing an assortment of promises, some material (tax cuts) and some philosophical (abortion), each important to some element in the party coalition, each of differing importance to the distinct members of the coalition.

Direct material gain is another type of coalitional goal. American parties have often been conceptualized as primarily concerned with such material goals as patronage, contracts, graft, office, and subsidies. These coalitional, rather than collective, goals were stressed in the concept of party advanced by another Democrat of Wilson's time:

> In two Presidential campaigns, the leaders talked themselves red in the face about silver bein' the best money and gold bein' no good, and they tried to prove it out of books. Do you think the people cared for all that guff? No. They heartily indorsed what Richard Crocker said: "What's the use of discussin' what's the best kind of money?" said Crocker. "I'm in favor of all kinds of money—the more the better." See how a real Tammany statesman can settle in twenty-five words a problem that monopolized two campaigns![20]

The third element composing concepts of parties is the mode employed by parties (see Figure 1.3). Mode involves a combination of the style,

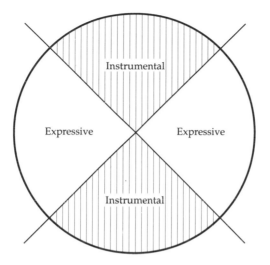

Figure 1.3. Concepts of Political Parties: Mode

incentives, and system of membership compensation of the party. Concepts of parties stress different modes, depending on whether the party is seen as either an instrumental means to other, more important goals or as a central expression of the members' political life. It is the difference between party as a tool and party as a faith.[21]

The instrumental party is calculating and rational—it provides direct compensation to its workers and makes appeals to the interests of voters. Modern campaign consultants serve as almost a pure example; in their emphasis on the technical arts of campaigning, they see emotion and public policies as a means to win office, not as inherently valuable.[22] Anthony Downs provides a good example of the instrumental mode in party theory. Parties have no principled core in his model but are axiomatically defined as a "team" of politicians who seek "to control the governing apparatus by gaining office in a duly constituted election." Assuming the parties to be concerned only with the rewards of office, Downs builds his impressive theory on one basic hypothesis: "Parties formulate policies in order to win elections, rather than win elections in order to formulate policies."[23]

In the expressive mode, parties are more essential to their adherents' emotional life than to their material well-being. With their affective roots, these parties are likely to evidence strong internal solidarity, personal and group loyalties, and broad ideologies. More than a political entity, the expressive party is a community, "a spiritual proximity, a kind of consanguinity of minds, which discover a certain nearness and resemblance between themselves."[24] The expressive party is impassioned—it provides intangible rewards to its workers and makes affective appeals to voters. Its programs will not emphasize calculating appeals to particularistic groups, e.g., an increase in social security pensions, but emotional entreaties, e.g., a call for the unity of the devout or of the working class. The rewards of politics are found primarily in purposive incentives, sometimes with the added attraction of social, but still collective, benefits.[25]

The expressive mode of politics has been evident occasionally in American parties, especially when they have been the instrument of broad social movements, or at times among minor parties. The fullest model of an expressive party, however, comes not from America but from Russia's Lenin.

To Lenin, party organization required dedicated, professional revolutionaries. When competing for power within liberal democracies, an expressive party becomes increasingly necessary, for "the more widely the masses are drawn into the struggle and form the basis of the movement, the more necessary it is to have such an organization and the more stable must it be."[26] Despite its recent failures, the Leninist concept has inspired parties worldwide.

PARTY CONCEPTS

A full concept of a political party combines these three dimensions, resulting in a particular viewpoint on party focus, goals, and mode. Eight concepts of political parties result from the combination of these three dimensions. For an illustration of the combinations and an abstract type of political party that would exemplify each combination, see Figure 1.4 and Table 1.1.

The party as bureaucratic organization is a common concept, highlighting the party's hierarchical structure, professionalism, and orientation toward the goal of electoral victory. Michels, the founding father of modern organizational theory,[27] is foremost in the elaboration of the concept, but practicing politicians such as Martin Van Buren have also developed this party model. The concept seems increasingly applicable as the parties develop professional staffs, large financial resources, and technical expertise.

The party as governing caucus is the party of Burke and Wilson and a

Table 1.1. Political Party Concepts

	Collective Goals Mode		Coalitional Goals Mode	
	Instrumental	Expressive	Instrumental	Expressive
Elite focus	Governing caucus	Ideological community	Bureaucratic organization	Urban machine
Mass focus	Cause advocate	Social movement	Rational team of office seekers	Personal faction

favored model of party reformers, such as a famous committee of the American Political Science Association.[28] These parties are elite groups, which seek collective goals and employ the instrumental mode. Alternatively, with a mass focus, this party has a counterpart in the concept of party as cause advocate. Ostrogorski urges this model most forcefully, in his argument for single-issue parties.[29]

Two concepts deal with parties seeking collective goals and employing the expressive mode. When focused on its elite, this party is an ideological community, a "gemeinschaft," a party that encompasses strong interpersonal bonds among its adherents as it seeks broad social transformation. This is the ideal that Lenin elaborated and that Michels later sought among Italian Fascists. As this party turns to mass action, it seeks to create a social movement, in which politics is expressive of an encompassing ideology beyond the immediate interests of the partisans. In the United States, its character is evident among the Populists, Progressives, and other third parties.

The urban machine is a different kind of party. In the extensive studies of this form, analysts usually emphasize its material reward structure. Yet the success and regular reappearance of the machine form of party cannot be explained by emphasizing material rewards, particularly in an era when such rewards have been sharply diminished. Rather, the more basic appeal of the machine is expressive, the emotional ties it creates resting on the bases of ethnic loyalties, personal friendships, and neighborhood solidarity.

The model of party as a rational team of officeseekers employs the utilitarian theories of Jeremy Bentham and Anthony Downs. Adopting Bentham's assumptions of a calculating, utility-maximizing citizenry, Downs then elaborates the party's instrumental interactions with the electorate. In the expressive mode, the match of the rational team is the party as personal faction. In contemporary times, most typically, the loyalty in this mass-focused party will be to an individual candidate and his or her campaign organization.

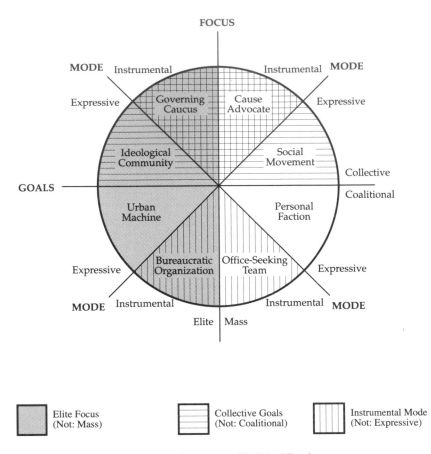

Figure 1.4. Concepts of Political Parties

PARTIES AND DEMOCRACY

Parties contribute to democracy, and party concepts can contribute to democratic theory. Theories of democracy are alike only in their premise that legitimate government must rest on a mass base. Beyond this common premise, the most diverse forms of politics have grasped the mantle of democracy. Authoritarian rulers claim to speak in the name of the people and to interpret their "true" democratic will. Advocates of "participatory democracy" look to an extension of traditional town meetings, just as sponsors of referendums promote "direct democracy."

These ambiguities are even more pointed when we consider the modern nation-state. In contemporary times, the large size of the polity necessitates

Table 1.2. Party Concepts and Democracy

	Collective Goals Participation		Coalitional Goals Participation	
	Limited	Extensive	Limited	Extensive
Autonomous leadership	Governing caucus	Ideological community	Bureaucratic organization	Urban machine
Accessible leadership	Cause advocate	Social movement	Rational team of office seekers	Personal faction

representative, rather than direct, democracy. Since government "of the people" cannot be an unmediated government "by the people," how do we make possible government "for the people"? To what extent should we promote and to what extent limit the connection between the representatives and their constituents?

Three dimensions of democratic theory are particularly relevant: the accessibility of leadership, voter goals, and the character of participation. These dimensions parallel those used in classifying the concepts of political parties. The particular party concepts already defined reflect not only angles of vision on political parties but also views of democratic philosophies on the appropriate relationship of voters to party leaders, goals, and appeals. The congruence is depicted in Table 1.2 and Figure 1.5.

A critical element in democratic theory is the accessibility of leadership, as Kornhauser suggests.[30] Leaders may be considerably autonomous from the citizenry, or the rank and file may have ready means to select, remove, and control the party chieftains. The distinction is not absolute, but there certainly is a difference, for example, between a party in which party activists choose their own leaders (nineteenth-century presidential conventions) and a party in which a mass electorate makes the selection (contemporary presidential primaries).

The distinction is also evident today in the different ways in which election campaigns are conducted. Among different parties, popular attitudes may be more or less effective and legitimate in shaping campaign appeals. When the party is led by a team of office seekers, the electorate has ready access to the leadership because that leadership worries only about its possible electoral defeat. When a party becomes an organizational bureaucracy, however, party leadership takes on the autonomy of all bureaucracies. Its own interests receive increased attention, and the mass citizenry is confined to the role of a passive electorate.

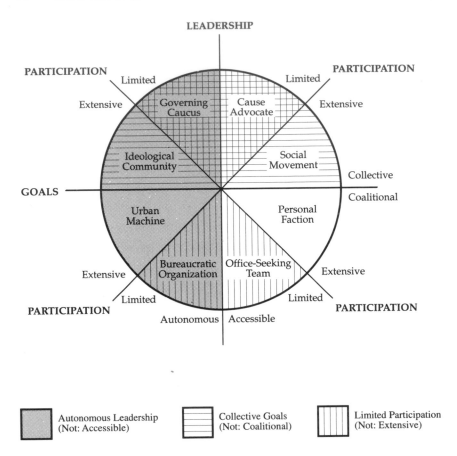

Figure 1.5. Political Parties and Democracy

Voter goals, the second dimension, parallel those of parties and can also be categorized as either collective or coalitional. We can ask whether voters do, or should, seek to promote their particular interests, joining coalitions with others when necessary, or whether they emphasize collective goals. Like our other categories, this is only a relative distinction. Surely voters give some attention to their particular interests—if they don't, who will?—but a society cannot exist if its members pursue only self-interests. To examine the distinction, we could study the appeals made to voters in elections. When voters are seen as an ideological community, the appeals will be phrased in broad visions of the public good. When voters are seen more narrowly, as utility maximizers, electoral programs will be collections of appeals to distinct interests.

A third major distinction among theories of democracy emerges in their emphasis on popular participation. Even though some mass involvement is basic to democracy, the extent, character, and asserted desirability of that participation can vary greatly. Indeed, Schumpeter's prominent definition sees democracy as simply a competition between elites.[31] Alternative concepts promote broader mass involvement, whether in nominating primaries, policy referenda, or even worker participation in industry. Party attitudes toward its membership illustrate the distinction. A governing caucus is inherently restrictive in membership; it sees voters as a resource to be used or courted to advance the interests and programs of the caucus but not as an integral element within the party. In contrast, the urban machine, when functioning well, enthusiastically recruits new membership and encourages wide participation (although not necessarily a wide sharing of power).

Different attitudes on the extent of popular participation also involve different attitudes on the character of that participation. When limited, involvement typically is restricted to the interests or policy preferences of the voters; when extensive, involvement will reach deeper emotional loyalties. The categories of this dimension thereby parallel the earlier distinction between the instrumental and expressive modes of the parties.

PARTIES AND POLITICAL SYSTEMS

We may go one tentative step further. The party concepts developed here have a potentially broader significance. Particular kinds of parties also fit with particular kinds of government and different concepts of democracy. Analyzing these relationships would require a major investigation of a different sort, but we can still speculate on the association between particular parties and particular polities.

This theoretical possibility is sketched in Table 1.3 and Figure 1.6. For example, the first (upper-left) cell of the table and the corresponding segment of the circular graph suggest that a governing caucus party would probably be most evident in a democracy considered as a trusteeship, in which its leaders are permitted to pursue their rational vision of the public good without close popular control. Significantly, Burke is the most prominent advocate of both the governing caucus model of parties and of the trusteeship theory of government.[32]

Table 1.3. Party Concepts and Political Systems

	Collective Goals Participation		Coalitional Goals Participation	
	Limited	Extensive	Limited	Extensive
Autonomous leadership	Trusteeship	Vanguard guidance	Elite competition	Patronage, consociation
Accessible leadership	Plebiscitary rule	Progressivism, direct democracy	Utilitarian individualism	Fascism

Alternative understandings of democracy are cited in the other cells of the table, each consistent with the corresponding party concept in the preceding tables. Thus, in some polities, elites employ mass arousal to legitimize their policy goals even while limiting broader popular participation. These systems can be characterized as examples of plebiscitary rule.

More extensive popular participation is expected in the two other models of democratic politics emphasizing collective goods. "Vanguard guidance" is an awkward term used to encompass justifications for authority by such diverse groups as the single-party systems of the developing world and the Communist parties in former "people's republics." Progressivism or direct democracy, in contrast, provides for direct popular involvement in the search for collective goods; its institutional expression comes in such devices as the initiative, referendum, and direct primary.

The more common forms of democracy, found on the right-hand side of the table, pursue coalitional goals. Schumpeter, expecting limited involvement from the electorate, presents a model of democracy as elite competition. Closer connections are expected in the Benthamite and Downsian theories of utilitarian individualism, with voters expected to be rational calculators of their personal advantages.

The ethnic and particularistic loyalties that sustain the urban machine are best reflected in governments that recognize these distinct social groupings. One variety, more common in developing nations, is politics conducted through powerful patrons. Another common democratic variety is consociation, with direct representation of religious and ethnic associations.[33]

Democratic legitimacy is also claimed, although falsely, by personalistic leaders, who arouse mass support to validate their claims as individual embodiments of the people's will. The twentieth century has seen too many

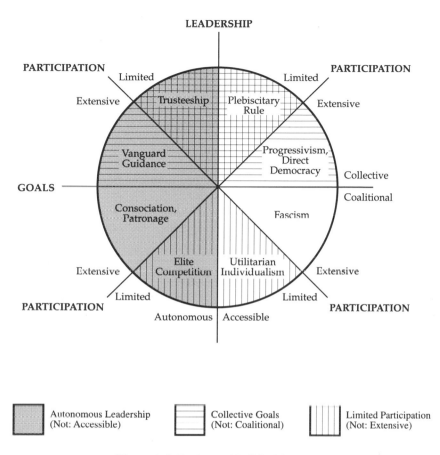

Figure 1.6. Parties and Political Systems

examples of such fascism, typified by Italy's Mussolini, Argentina's Peron, and Germany's Hitler.

ANALYZING PASSIONS AND INTERESTS

In the following chapters, I analyze the eight party models, compare them to American political experience, and discuss their implications for democratic theory and practice. I will consider the models separately and in each case raise problems for democracy that are inherent in these particular party models.

The concept of party as bureaucratic organization is examined in the next chapter. Bureaucracies can mobilize popular electorates, but they also are likely to limit the electorate to the role of spectator. This effect raises the vital theoretical issue of democratic participation.

The party as governing caucus is the principal subject of chapter 3, in which the party as cause advocate is also considered. In these parties, leadership is likely to become separated from its mass support, and citizen participation is stilted. Sustaining popular involvement is a continuing problem of democratic theory.

In chapter 4, I examine parties with collective goals that employ the expressive mode, the party as ideological community and as social movement. Although these parties are often seen as pristinely democratic, their ideological emphasis presents a potential problem of intolerant orthodoxy, unsuitable in democracy.

The urban machine is the subject of chapter 5. The machine's stimulation of mass attachment can promote democracy; however, its limited vision makes achieving important social goals difficult, and its emphasis on personal gain obstructs the true citizenship that is necessary for a full democracy.

In chapter 6, the final two concepts are considered, the party as a rational team of office seekers and the party as personal faction. These parties do devote considerable attention to mass demands, but in their individualistic assumptions they are prone to undermine the social responsibility necessary for effective democracy.

Having analyzed the eight party concepts, I then apply them to two aspects of American politics. In chapter 7, the theoretical expectations of voter behavior implicit in each of the party concepts are developed and then compared to the historical record and to empirical research on American voting behavior. For this purpose, the degree of mobilization, partisanship, issue orientation, and candidate appeals among the electorate are reviewed.

In chapter 8, I examine different programs for the reform of American parties, alternatives that are closely related to the basic party concepts. Depending on their initial assumptions, proposed reforms are directed toward very different goals, including progressive individualism, nonpartisanship, party government, and party efficiency.

In chapter 9, the conclusion, I restate the basic theme of the connection between political parties and modern democracy and examine the contribution of parties to democratic values as well as their place in the alternative theoretical traditions of liberal and communitarian democracy. I conclude with speculations on the future role of political parties in the United States and with proposals to strengthen the parties as institutions of American democracy.

Analyses of parties and of democracy inevitably overlap. Historically, and as recently as the peaceful revolutions in Eastern Europe and the Soviet Union, parties and democracy have been associated both in logic and in the world of events. We cannot divorce this intellectual pair; this book instead celebrates their continued union.

TWO
INTERESTS WITHOUT PASSIONS:
PARTY AS BUREAUCRATIC ORGANIZATION

It has been those who . . . refrained the most from suffering their personal
behavior from being inflamed by their political rivalries and were most willing
to leave the question of their individual advancement to the quiet and friendly
arbitrament of their political associates [who] have in the end been the most
successful.
—*Martin Van Buren*[1]

The fundamental sociological law of political parties may be formulated in the
following terms: "It is organization which gives birth to the dominion of the
elected over the electors, of the mandatories over the mandators, of the
delegates over the delegators."
—*Robert Michels*[2]

The eighth president of the United States and the first major theorist of
political parties lived a century apart and shared no common political culture. Still, they agreed in their theoretical concept of political parties. To
both men, a party would inevitably be a bureaucratic organization with an
elite focus, seeking coalitional goals and relying on instrumental appeals
by the party leadership. But they differed completely in their normative
assessments of the effect of such parties on democracy. Van Buren hailed
the bureaucratic party as necessary to effect popular government; Michels
saw it as fundamentally subversive of democracy.

These two writers came to their conclusions from very different perspectives. Van Buren developed his theories in reaction to the factional-
ized, personalized politics of the early nineteenth-century one-party "era
of good feelings." He saw party organization as necessary to achieve both
victory for his colleagues and appropriate public policies. Putting his theories into practice, he accomplished much: the creation of the Democratic
party, the election of Andrew Jackson, its first candidate for president, and
then his own elevation to the White House.[3]

Robert Michels reflected a different place and time, imperial Germany
before World War I. A Marxian and a Socialist, Michels became disillu-
sioned with his party's failure to win power and with its apparent abandonment of its radical program and egalitarian character. To explain these

failures, he developed his theory of the "iron law of oligarchy," the inevitable tendency of any organization—even one ideologically committed to socialist equality—to come under the control of a closed and conservative leadership. His pessimism deepened with the war, as Europe's working classes exuberantly marched to their mutual slaughter. Despairing of any possibility of true democracy, he eventually became a supporter of fascism in Mussolini's Italy.

PARTY AS BUREAUCRACY

The party as bureaucratic organization emphasizes coalitional goals. These typically include not only the power of office but also policy objectives, such as Van Buren's beliefs, derived from Jefferson, in states' rights rather than in strong national government or the German Socialist party's original Marxian ideology of proletarian revolution. Accomplishing these goals, however, first requires electoral victory.

In time, victory—meant to be a means to policy goals—replaces policy objectives as the primary objective of the party. Thus, Van Buren's party, "even though founded on Republican principles, became an anti-ideological force."[4] Similarly, among Michels's Socialists, there was "a continued increase in the prudence, the timidity even, which inspires its policy. The party doctrines are, whenever requisite, attenuated and deformed in accordance with the external needs of the organization."[5]

Pursuing the goal of victory, parties develop the characteristic features of bureaucracy. To wage successful combat against their electoral enemies, they must become hierarchical, obedient organizations. "The modern party is a fighting organization in the political sense of the term," Michels argues, "and must as such conform to the laws of tactics. . . . In a party, and above all in a fighting political party, democracy . . . is utterly incompatible with strategic promptness, and the forces of democracy do not lend themselves to the rapid opening of a campaign."[6]

With this emphasis on combat, political parties are often described in military language—not only in Germany but also in nineteenth-century America. Parties were "organized, officered, drilled, manipulated, fitted to work consistently for power with inconsistent principles."[7] And Richard Jensen depicts post–Civil War politics:

Parties were like armies fighting at the polls for the spoils of victory. Politicians were like generals—many had been generals or colonels in the war—whose strategy was to whip up enthusiasm among the rank and file. Parades, speechfests, all-day picnics, and continuous door-to-door solicitation maximized interest and minimized the risks of defections.[8]

The bureaucratic party shares with a military bureaucracy an emphasis on internal discipline; orders are given and must be obeyed in pursuit of victory. As Van Buren's associate commanded his partisan leaders, "Tell them they are safe if they fear the enemy, but that the first man we see *step to the rear*, we *cut down* . . . they *must* not falter, or they perish."[9] Van Buren's party developed a centralized command, the Albany Regency, which would implement its decisions through local councils of the party and mass mobilization. "After the dominant clique of the party arrived at a decision, the information was ultimately transmitted to the legislators, newspapers, and politicians. Rallies and public meetings were sponsored to popularize the policy."[10]

To assure discipline, the bureaucratic party relies on individual, material rewards. The most conspicuous in American politics has been patronage, the filling of public offices on the basis of party service. William Marcy defended his allies in the Van Buren organization: "They boldly preach what they practice. When they are contending for victory, they avow their intention of enjoying the fruits of it. . . . If they are successful, they claim, as a matter of right, the advantages of success. They see nothing wrong in the rule, that to the victor belong the spoils of the enemy."[11]

Appointments to party positions, as well as to public office, are also important, in Michels's view, in strengthening leaders within the party bureaucracy. These leaders recruit new talent into the party, as "the influence which they exercise and the financial security of their position become more and more fascinating to the masses, stimulating the ambition of all the more talented elements to enter the privileged bureaucracy of the labor movement." Patronage can also be used to placate potential foes within the party: "The leaders of the opposition receive high office and honors in the party, and are thus rendered innocuous—all the more so seeing that they are not admitted to the supreme offices."[12]

In later years, patronage would come into disrepute, restricted by civil service laws, self-protective administrative agencies, and the courts. Even in modern times, however, it could still find a few champions, such as Supreme Court Justice Lewis Powell. Dissenting in a case restricting patronage appointments, he echoed earlier endorsements of the bureaucratic party's individualistic rewards: "Patronage appointments help build stable political parties by offering rewards to persons who assume the tasks necessary to the continued functioning of political organizations."[13] (We will return to this discussion in chapter 8.)

Although these parties use personal patronage, the important feature of any bureaucracy is its emphasis on coalitional victory, not individual rewards. Its campaign is directed toward the success of the entire party, not any individual's or even any combination of individuals. When personal interests become predominant, the pattern Michels criticized among the German Socialists, the party has been perverted, becoming more of a personal coalition than a party bureaucracy.

More in keeping with the model was Van Buren's behavior, subordinating individual claims to party goals. In place of the personal factions of individual leaders typical in his day, he saw a political party as the agency of broader interests. Thus, the New Yorker organized Jackson's successful presidential bid in 1828, not principally for personal gain but "because he could use the General to reform the party, eliminate Federalist principles from the national government, and oust [John Quincy] Adams from office."[14]

When Van Buren himself later ran for president, his candidacy was based on his party leadership, not on his individual characteristics. The emphasis was evident in the Democrats' protoplatform in 1836: It mentioned Van Buren's name only once, cited other party leaders thirty-two times, and referred to the party itself most frequently, in thirty-four instances.[15]

Bureaucracies, including parties, have two different aspects.[16] They ostensibly exist to perform a particular task—in the case of parties, to achieve electoral victory. They are also social systems, however, involving affective and psychological relationships both among their members and between the bureaucracy and its external world. Michels understood this second relationship and saw psychological influences as major causes of inevitable oligarchy within parties. They included "the tendency of the leaders to organize themselves and to consolidate their interests, . . . the gratitude of the led towards the leaders, and the general immobility and passivity of the masses [all reinforcing] the technical indispensability of leadership."[17]

Affective relationships, inevitable in any bureaucracy, can also have beneficial effects. In Van Buren's party, democratic relationships were fostered among the leadership, who made decisions jointly. By insisting on a united front, participants subordinated their individual interests to the perceived general interest of the party.[18]

On the federal level, Van Buren's party was able to overcome sectional rivalries, develop the most truly national coalition yet evident in America, and stimulate a competitive party system that was balanced and competitive on the state, regional, and national levels. [19] On the individual level, Van Buren's party democracy taught an important "moral discipline, putting a high premium upon loyalty, fidelity, patriotism, and self-restraint."[20] By extending its organization at the local level, it taught its partisans also to be citizens. Their heritage is the model of party as bureaucratic organization.

THE CONTEMPORARY PARTY BUREAUCRACY

Abstract concepts differ from empirical reality, and thus a comparison of the model of party as a bureaucratic organization to contemporary American parties is in order. These parties increasingly evidence the character of bureaucracies, but basic environmental factors of American politics limit their bureaucratic character.

A bureaucracy manifests such features as specialization of labor, professional expertise, hierarchical organization, objective and internal recruitment of leadership, and the availability of resources. These features are directed toward particular objectives, most importantly the achievement of designated tasks and the maintenance of the bureaucracy itself. Bureaucracies exist both in government and in the private world—the civil service and the modern corporation are similar organizations; even their purposes may be as similar as providing social security benefits or selling retirement annuities.

On both the state and the national levels, American parties have become more bureaucratic. Reviewing the development of state party organizations over two decades, the authors of a major study argue that "party organizational change in a period of profound concern for the future of parties has been in the direction of strengthening the organizational attributes of individual party units, and the patterns of relationships among the units."[21] To test the character of state parties, the authors use a series of indicators of strength for the party bureaucracy. These include a permanent headquarters; autonomous powers of state chairpersons; large full-time and long-term staffs with specialized divisions of labor; a variety of institutional support activities (e.g., voter mobilization and publication of a newsletter); a variety of activities in support of candidates (e.g., campaign seminars and polling); and significant party spending. Some of these indicators certainly show an increase in the capacity of state parties as bureaucratic organizations. Illustratively, in the early 1960s only half of the Democratic state parties had even a single full-time, professional employee, and only one-third conducted a state voter-mobilization campaign. By 1980, 85 percent of the Democratic state parties had some full-time staff, and two-thirds conducted voter campaigns.

Republicans were more fully organized in both time periods. Even in the 1960s more than two-thirds of their state parties had some full-time staff, and six out of ten had voter programs. By 1980 party bureaucratization had progressed so that virtually every Republican state organization had professional staff, and eight of ten conducted voter mobilization.[22]

These changes, however, still leave the state parties as only limited bureaucracies. The average number of full-time staff, for example, was only 4.5 for Democratic organizations, and 7.0 for Republicans—scarcely measures of elaborate bureaucracies. Moreover, party organizational development appears to have slowed or reversed in more recent years, particularly among Democrats. Even over the longer period, there is some reason to doubt bureaucratic growth if we examine party spending, perhaps the most reliable indicator because it is measured in hard coin. Party budgets actually decreased during this period, once inflation is taken into account.[23]

The national parties have become extensive bureaucracies in their own right and are more impressive than the state organizations. "Contemporary national party organizations are larger, better financed, more stable, and more internally diversified than ever before. In a word, they have become institutionalized."[24] Among them, the six leading bureaucracies of the major parties (national, senatorial, and congressional committees of each of the two parties) spent total budgets of $209 million in the nonpresidential period of 1989–1990. In direct campaign spending, this amount represented more than a fourfold increase over the previous twelve years.[25]

These national organizations now bear all the marks of a true bureaucracy. Their staffs are relatively long-term, professional, and large, numbered in the hundreds, and housed in permanent party buildings in Washington. They engage in general party activity, such as issues research; provide financial and administrative help to state and local organizations, in the process reversing the traditional subordination of the national parties; furnish extensive help to individual candidates, including recruitment, training, polling, and media production; and provide both direct funds and financial brokerage between contributors and candidates.

This bureaucratic development is probably the most significant change in contemporary American politics. Moreover, these are national bureaucracies that may well diminish the traditional decentralization of U.S. parties. This change was probably inevitable as the nation itself became centralized. "Strong national party organizations," Epstein concludes, "are new American phenomena. Now that they have finally begun to be substantial, it is easy to believe that they are here to stay and their previous absence was an anomaly in a political and social system already predominantly national in so many other respects."[26] The new national parties reflect basic changes in American life, such as the shift to a cash economy in politics and the parallel dependence on campaigning through the mass media. The nature of American politics, however, imposes inherent limits on the bureaucratization of the parties.

THE LIMITS OF BUREAUCRACY

Leadership is the most vital aspect of any organization. Typically, bureaucracies seek internal control of the selection of leadership by imposing professional standards of expertise for recruitment and ultimately for the choice of top managers. To illustrate, an educational bureaucracy will insist that only experienced teachers can be school principals or superintendents. The claims of expertise can also be raised in a party bureaucracy, as Michels observed: "In proportion as the profession of politician becomes a more complicated one, and in proportion as the rules of social legislation become more numerous, it is necessary for one who would understand politics to possess wider experience and more extensive knowledge."[27]

Party bureaucracies in the United States, however, ultimately cannot select their own leadership. The real head of an American party bureaucracy is the elected executive of the constituency—the governor for a state party, the president for a national party. The formal chairs of these organizations are in effect not only named by the elected politician but dependent for their power on his or her favor.[28] If party bureaucracies controlled the selection of public officials, this dependency would be only a formal relationship, equivalent to the formal power of the British king to name the prime minister. In reality, the bureaucracies lack this control, for they neither nominate nor elect officials bearing the party label. Since virtually all party nominations are made in primaries, candidates can—and do—win the party designation without support from the party bureaucracy. Indeed, running against the "party bosses" is a common and often successful practice.

The freedom of candidates from party control is even more dramatically evident on the national level. With the extension of primaries, presidential campaigns are conducted entirely by individual candidates, who bypass state organizations to make direct appeals to interest groups, contributors, and individual voters. The national committees do not participate in these contests—they only set the rules or provide services impartially to all candidates (even shared opinion polls). They do not enter the arena of the struggle but passively await capture as secondary prizes of victory.

Nor, once candidates are nominated, do party bureaucracies control their election. Although party committees are increasingly active in services to candidates, the dominant role is held by the candidates themselves. Technology, particularly television and computerized campaigning, has permanently established "the ability of politicians to affect their own destinies. Parties thus can be only as important as candidates permit them to be."[29] Even when parties are important initially, once candidates are elected they develop their own strengths as incumbents and become increasingly self-sufficient.

Money, the crucial resource of contemporary politics, precisely measures the relationship. Although the parties have increased their financial role, it is still quite limited since the overwhelming proportion of campaign contributions, particularly for incumbents, comes from individual donors or from political action committees. For example, in 1989–1990, total spending for the congressional elections was $445 million, of which only 5 percent came directly from the six nationwide party committees.[30]

The role of the party bureaucracies is further limited inherently by the structure of American elections. Elections are extraordinarily diffuse, comprising some ten thousand partisan offices just on the state and national levels and hundreds of thousands of local offices; moreover, for most of these positions there are nominating primaries. Both primaries and general elections are easily entered by candidates and easily influenced by voters uncommitted to the party. A bureaucracy seeking to control these multitudinous elections is likely to suffer from overload or breakdown.

Still another complication is that these elections are considerably distinct from one another in time and space. The contests for separate offices may be held at different times of the year and on different cycles so that a typical community may have spring elections for municipal offices, summer primaries, and fall general elections, with terms of office encompassing different periods of one, two, or four years. Furthermore, the geographical constituencies are distinct—the boundaries of a congressional district do not necessarily coincide with those of state legislative districts or even with those of local towns and cities. Conducting elections in these conditions is a daunting task for a party bureaucracy, akin to General Motors trying to convince the same customer to buy a Chevrolet *and* a Pontiac *and* an Oldsmobile and to buy them at different times in the same year.

A bureaucracy also seeks permanence and regularity, but the electoral calendar undermines these goals. Political activity in the United States has a troublesome periodic ebb and flow. Like a seasonal business, a party bureaucracy will have its busy and slack periods; in a party, however, the temporal cycles of activity are more difficult to manage than in a seasonal business. Because elections occur at fixed periods (unlike parliamentary parties, which may face an election at any time), the party has no need to maintain its staff continually, limiting its efficiency. Moreover, the two-year and four-year cycles between the major contests for state and national offices are so long that the party bureaucracy will suffer repeated expansions and contractions in size, activity, and opportunities to sharpen skills. It is as if baseball players had pennant races only every other year; would such teams be cohesive and disciplined?

Party bureaucracies, like others, require resources, especially skilled personnel and money—money that can also buy skills. In the more traditional party bureaucracy of Van Buren, the most important resources were individual local campaigners with strong interpersonal skills. The party secured this resource through patronage, which amounted to a hidden public subsidy to the parties. In contemporary times, patronage is less respected and less common; even where it remains, studies have shown that in practice patronage employees are not hired, rewarded, or punished on the basis of their contributions to the party.[31] Patronage is no longer used effectively by the parties to promote bureaucratic goals.

For reasons to be considered in chapter 5, patronage always had severe limitations. In contemporary politics, it is even less useful, as the nation has shifted from labor-intensive to capital-intensive politics. The skills now required—such as media or polling expertise—are of a different order and must be purchased through direct and substantial cash payments rather than through low-paying jobs with indirect benefits of friendship or graft. Parties, however, have no assured sources of cash nor any substantial public subsidies; their bureaucratic development is consequently always uncertain.

In the end, parties cannot be full-scale bureaucracies because they lack a bureaucratic environment. The ideal bureaucracy lives in a closed world, where it controls its internal life, operates by fixed and impersonal rules, and relates to outsiders as uncontrolling clients. In its beneficial aspect, a bureaucracy behaves like an impartial judiciary; in its pathological aspect, it becomes the rule-bound tribunal depicted in Franz Kafka's novel, *The Trial*.

Parties, however, are ultimately dependent on different, external controls. They must meet the tests of elections and are subject to the wishes or whims of the voters. They operate in a political marketplace, not in a closed bureaucratic environment. To this extent, they are more similar to economic competitors such as corporations.[32] Like corporations, they must be assessed by their results, not by their bureaucratic neatness. As the corporation judges its success ultimately by the market test of profits, the party must judge its success by the market test of votes. On these grounds, bureaucratic development is not always beneficial to parties. State parties that are stronger by bureaucratic standards, for example, show hardly any greater ability to win elections.[33] It may be that hierarchical, self-contained bureaucracies are ill-adapted to the dispersed nature of the American electoral system.

BUREAUCRACY AND DEMOCRACY

The critical issue, however, is not the organizational effectiveness of party bureaucracies but their possible contribution to effective democracy. In their most evident features, bureaucracy and democracy would seem to be incompatible.

Bureaucracy emphasizes the specialized knowledge of the expert; democracy assumes that all men and women are sufficiently knowledgeable to share in decisionmaking. The first is characteristically hierarchical; the second stresses equality among persons. Bureaucracy focuses on limited, organizational tasks, but democracy concerns the general and common political interests of the populace. A bureaucratic organization relies on paid labor, but a democratic organization assumes its members will volunteer time and effort.

Political parties that follow the model of a bureaucratic organization may merit democratic suspicion, as Michels argues. Leadership in a bureaucratic party typically differs from the rank and file in perspective. For followers, the party is a means to such ends as public policies or group satisfactions; leaders tend to see the maintenance and success of the party as itself the primary goal. "From a means, organization becomes an end. To the institutions and qualities which at the outset were destined simply to ensure the good working of the party machine . . . greater importance comes ultimately to be attached than to the productivity of the machine. . . . As the party's need for tranquillity increases, its revolutionary talons atrophy."[34]

Party bureaucrats also may have somewhat different interests from their followers or the voters. As experts in politics, they come to share a craft and a professional technical specialization across parties that can become more important than their ostensible ideological differences. For example, at postelection conferences sponsored by Harvard's Kennedy School of Government, rival campaign managers meet to evaluate strategies, slogans, and advertisements for their electoral impact, ignoring party programs and philosophies.[35] For these leading party bureaucrats, the art of politics replaces its substance.

There also are more immediate interests. A party bureaucrat "lives 'off' politics as a vocation," and "strives to make politics a permanent source of income."[36] Party bureaucrats are always, even if not always primarily, jobholders. Even if they are ideologically committed to the party cause, they need to protect their jobs, promoting their particular economic interests, such as higher pay or career mobility, that may not parallel the party's more general goals.

In a political organization, moreover, power itself becomes an individual psychological reward apart from the party's interests. Michels's observation of the German working class may be true of all party careerists: "For them, the loss of their positions would be a financial disaster, and in most cases it would be impossible for them to return to their old way of life. They have been spoiled for any other work than that of propaganda. Their hands have lost the callosities of the manual toiler, and are likely to suffer only from writer's cramp."[37]

Party bureaucrats are also likely to be inaccessible to control by the rank and file. Possessed of skills necessary to the party, bureaucrats cannot be easily dismissed; unelected, they cannot be voted out of office. Control depends greatly on the bureaucrats' own devotion to their party. Self-interested, they cannot be trusted always to further the party's goals. Even when conscientiously seeking victory for the party, they may subvert its program.

A more general problem with party bureaucracy is its potential effect on democratic participation. In the bureaucratic model, the electorate is a resource to be mined for votes, not an integral element within the party itself. Carried to its logical conclusion, this perspective legitimizes the manipulation of voters in order to win elections. Contrasting their own political expertise and commitment to the voters' limited knowledge and sporadic involvement, bureaucrats can easily come to disparage voters and then to exploit their alleged "weakness for everything which appeals to their eyes and for such spectacles as will always attract a gaping crowd."[38]

Even when more gentle, however, party bureaucracy is likely to limit citizens' involvement. With its emphasis on efficiency, bureaucracy is prone to centralize authority, lessening the opportunities for individual and local activity. Because of its internal focus, voters are placed outside the party as spectators of the political struggle, not as participants, as audiences of political debate, not as debaters. A bureaucratic model, as McWilliams observes, defines "the party as a species of private property and voters as political consumers" and restricts the public to "an interest in the product but not in the process." For the citizenry, party becomes relevant only as a guide to periodic voting decisions but marginal to community life.[39]

Despite these many problems, bureaucratic parties may contribute to democracy. At its root, democracy means that ordinary people can affect government, but ordinary people must join together to be effective. Those people who have individual wealth, status, and power can sometimes take care of themselves, but "organization, based as it is upon the principle of least effort . . . is the weapon of the weak in their struggle with the strong.''[40] Parties, led by bureaucracies, can be the expression of political mobilization.

To achieve mobilization, a bureaucracy must be not simply an agency of technicians but a group with some commitments of its own. With such commitments, party bureaucrats can act as the vital links between mass opinion and public policy. Increasingly, in fact, the leaders of American parties are assuming this role, even as they become more electorally efficient.[41]

The contribution of party bureaucracy to democracy is still more basic in its stimulation of electoral participation. Voting turnout depends on many factors, including registration laws and demographic characteristics. Turnout is closely related to party efforts also; where parties are active, voting participation increases, particularly among groups of lower socioeconomic status. Party mobilization thus promotes democratic equality of access among the population. Historically, the close relationship can be seen in the United States: When parties were stronger, voting turnout was high; as the parties have weakened, turnout has declined, The same relationship is evident today, not only within the country but in international comparisons as well. Among the major democracies of the world, the United States has the lowest level of voter participation even though its citizens show relatively high levels of political sophistication and interest. One significant element in explaining this discrepancy is the limited degree of party mobilization.[42]

Party bureaucracies not only can stimulate voting; they can also make that voting more meaningful. Van Buren's party bureaucracy was important because it made parties more than the personal followings of a dominant leader and more than closed caucuses of the self-interested. Although self-interest was certainly a motive, the New Yorker exemplified how a party bureaucracy could broaden the popular base of politics, bringing new voters to the polls and new meaning to the vote. As Van Buren's party-building efforts illustrate, a bureaucracy can democratize politics on an individual level through the opportunities it creates. In their ideal form, bureaucracies recruit talent on the basis of merit, not ascribed or inherited status. Even Michels acknowledged that the Socialist party had provided new, although wasted, opportunities for political leadership by the German working class.

In Van Buren's America, the Democratic party became a vehicle for social mobility among new classes. One critic grudgingly acknowledged that party politics "provided a ladder for the 'new men' who had not enough influence and, perhaps, merit to climb up of themselves."[43] In place of the traditional landed aristocrats, there emerged more democratic, "modern political professionals who loved the bonhomie of political gatherings, a coterie of more-or-less equals who relied for success not on the authority of a brilliant charismatic leader but on their solidarity, patience and discipline."[44]

Party bureaucracy also can promote democracy more generally. Even at a minimal level of participation, it serves democracy by making political opposition legitimate. Given its many social divisions, the United States has been particularly wary of political conflict and apt to agree with George Washington that parties serve but to "render alien to each other those who ought to be bound together by fraternal affection."[45] Yet professional politicians like Van Buren take a different attitude toward parties, urging the nation "to recognize their necessity, to give them the credit they deserve, and to devote ourselves to improve and to elevate the principles and objects of our own and to support it ingenuously and faithfully."[46] Because it has a self-interest in promoting conflict, a party bureaucracy renders opposition as acceptable to the society and thereby provides even a passive electorate with a choice of contenders for power.

A party organization's contributions can go still further by enlisting persons into more active participation in politics. One means is through party principles, which give citizens an understanding of public issues, even when they are distorted by campaign rhetoric. To both Michels and Van Buren, the ultimate purpose of a party is to promote its ideological principles. Only a program can give direction to a party, they agreed, but only a party can mobilize majorities in support of a program.

Withal, party bureaucracies are still limited in their contributions to democracy because of their doubtful ability to arouse passions. In its more extensive forms, a party engages not only voters' heads but their hearts. It provides a source of allegiance deeper than programmatic conviction, forged in conflicts with the common enemy, able to withstand division and defeat. These affective loyalties are difficult for party bureaucracies; emotions seem to conflict with their rationalist task orientations.

In any organization, to be sure, affective loyalties do develop, but they are likely to be directed inwardly toward preserving the social relations within the group and to exclude those not regularly engaged on the job. Extending these emotional bounds will occur only when entrance to the group is open and participation is simple. Organizations do not often evidence these characteristics, but they can exist. The extensive local committee structure of the Van Buren party promoted affective bonds in its day, just as the decentralized and participatory Japanese factory does today; in both cases, significantly, affection has promoted organizational success. Contemporary centralized bureaucracies may also be successful, but they will not be loved.

The ultimate problem for a party bureaucracy is that it will be only a bureaucracy, that it will develop the characteristic pathologies and lose the compensating advantages of organization. Its opportunity for social advancement may become a closed door, its task orientation a soulless striving for success, and its affective support a resource for emotional manipulation.

To achieve the good and avoid the evils of party bureaucracy, we must remember Michels's fatalistic yet hopeful admonition: "The democratic currents of history resemble successive waves. They break ever on the same shoal. They are ever renewed. This enduring spectacle is simultaneously encouraging and depressing."[47]

THREE

COMMON INTERESTS: PARTY AS GOVERNING CAUCUS AND CAUSE ADVOCATE

As he took the presidential oath of office in 1913, Woodrow Wilson felt partisan pride in his Democratic party's newly won control of power in both houses of Congress and in the executive branch. To him, the election results meant "a change in government . . . much more than the mere success of a party." Indeed, Wilson declared, Democratic victory at the polls "means little except when the Nation is using that party for a large and definite purpose."[1]

Over fifty years later, in 1965, Lyndon Johnson spoke before Congress as a newly elected president. Having asked the electorate to approve his party program, he now asked a Democratic Congress to fulfill the presumed popular mandate for action toward a "Great Society." By 1981, another president, Ronald Reagan, spoke in parallel language to another Congress in favor of an opposite ideology. Invoking the election returns, he urged a legislature of divided party control to enact a Republican program of reduced taxation and more limited government.

Each of these presidents succeeded in changing the course of American public policy. Each argued, at least implicitly, from a conception of the political party as a governing caucus. To each, a political party was predominantly an elite grouping of professional politicians who pursued a broad, collective program and won support by its instrumental appeals. Their common conception of democracy was that of autonomous leadership, controlled by an electorate whose participation was limited to judgments on the leaders' collective programs.

The theory is attractive, its appeal demonstrated by its recurrence in American politics, including legislative programs by presidents and academic arguments by political scientists favoring "a more responsible two-party system." Despite this appeal, problems associated with the concept are also recurrent; only infrequently do American political parties empirically behave as governing caucuses. That empirical record suggests limitations to this concept, found both in its underlying theory of democracy and in the environment of American politics.

A RECURRING MODEL

Party as governing caucus is evident in Burke's famous definition of the party as "a body of men united . . . upon some particular principle." The English statesman and philosopher argued against the dominant eighteenth-century belief that parties were selfish and even unpatriotic. Burke described parties more nobly. Instead of their intrigue, he portrayed their unity; instead of a search for personal reward, he saw an effort to achieve programs of public benefit. Burke's intellectual descendants have included many Americans; like him, they praised their party instead of apologizing for their partisanship.

In 1944, commemorating the founding of the Republican party, Wendell Willkie declared,

> One of the major functions of a political party is to give men of conviction a platform from which to argue their cause both within the party and outside it. . . . These leaders must convince the people, not that the party has been right in the past, but that it can be right, that it will be right in the future. A political party is an indispensable vehicle for men who offer themselves for office. Yet it is an equally indispensable vehicle for ideas and for the advocacy of principles.[2]

A later Republican, Ronald Reagan, would agree, in his description of the 1984 presidential campaign: "America is presented with the clearest political choice of half a century. The distinctions between our two parties and the different philosophy of our political opponents are at the heart of this campaign and America's future."[3]

Wilson's inaugural address is particularly noteworthy for its partisan character. The typical speech at this civic ritual emphasizes the unity of the nation, as in Jefferson's hopeful declaration, "We are all Federalists, we are all Republicans." Wilson, in contrast, began his masterful speech with a recitation of Democratic election victories and justified them with a new moral "vision of our life as a whole":

> With this vision we approach new affairs. . . . The scales of heedlessness have fallen from our eyes. We have made up our minds to square every process of our national life again with the standards we

so proudly set up at the beginning and have always carried at our hearts. Our work is a work of restoration.[4]

A former professor of political science, Wilson was most precise in articulating the concept of party as a governing caucus. To Wilson, a political party drew its social purpose from its policy program. It should create appropriate institutions to achieve that program—in the American context, a programmatic caucus in Congress led by a populist president. It should draw the legitimacy for this program from election mandates, and it should be rejected when it strayed from these policy goals.

Wilson saw the political party as a means of achieving collective responsibility in a democracy. This collective character went far beyond the view of party as a "team of office seekers." Indeed, Wilson was rather disdainful of professional politicians, a trait that would cause him trouble in his career. "I am not interested in men," he admitted, even while campaigning for his own election as president. "I must frankly say, without apologies, that I am not interested in the candidates of the other parties, and I find it difficult to get interested in the candidate of my own party because the thing to be done is so much bigger than men."[5]

Individual politicians could be disregarded because as individuals they could never effect a national program, even if each legislator slavishly followed his local constituency. Similarly, disaggregated elections could never achieve true popular control: "There are so many cooks mixing their ingredients in the national broth that it seems hopeless, this theory of changing one cook at a time."[6] Meaning more than just elections, democracy to Wilson "consists essentially in the popular choice of and control over alternate groups of collectively responsible public officials,"[7] and more pointedly, "representative government is government by majorities, and government by majorities is party government, which up to the present date is the only known means of self-government."[8]

Wilson sought means to institutionalize party government and turned first to Congress, in his day the dominant institution in the national government. Legislation there was controlled by the multiple and distinct subcommittees, unified only by the caucus of the party, convened "whenever, in critical seasons of doubt, it is necessary to assure itself of its own unity of purpose."

To make Congress the vehicle of party government, he proposed to use the caucus, even though it was "a very ugly beast, and a very unmanageable one." Strong leadership was needed, for this caucus "will obey only the strong hand, and heed only the whip. To rail against him is no good. He must be taken sternly in hand, and be harnessed, whether he will or not in our service. Our search must be for the bit that will curb and subdue him."[9]

Few people, and even fewer political scientists, have the opportunity to put their speculative proposals into practice. Wilson used his opportunity to institutionalize the concept of party as governing caucus. In the first two years of his administration, the congressional Democratic caucus was transformed from an ugly beast to a docile carrier of legislative burdens, enacting major programs such as the Clayton Anti-Trust Act and the lowered Underwood-Simons tariff.

Wilson not only used the caucus but also acted as the leader of his party. Presidential leadership became for Wilson the means to overcome the institutional separation of powers. To focus public and political attention on his program, Wilson used innovative techniques such as press conferences and personal delivery of the State of the Union address, previously submitted in writing. To strengthen his claim to leadership, he called for nomination of the president through direct popular primaries.

In later years, Wilson turned from Congress to the presidency to provide party government. The president "cannot escape being the leader of his party except by incapacity and lack of personal force, because he is at once the choice of the party and of the nation," Wilson had written as a professor, foreshadowing both his own leadership and his own disability. Though disdainful of personalities, he argued for the force of the person of the president: "He can dominate his party by being spokesman for the real sentiment and purpose of the country, by giving direction to opinion, by giving the country at once the information and the statements of policy which will enable it to form its judgments alike of parties and of men."[10] Through his actions and his rhetoric, the professor-cum-politician spurred a transformation of the presidency.[11]

Wilson's efforts have inspired other advocates of the model of party as governing caucus. In academic literature, the most notable has been the report of a Committee on Political Parties, presented to the American Political Science Association in 1950. Its program still constitutes the basic components of this model, requiring "first, that the parties are able to bring forth programs to which they commit themselves and, second, that the parties possess sufficient internal cohesion to carry out these programs."[12]

THE MODEL IN PRACTICE

I shall use this report, despite its age, to analyze the governing caucus model. Parties do affect government, yet they do not meet the full requirements of party as a governing caucus. To validate the governing caucus model, three conditions are necessary: Parties develop programs, they win election on the basis of these programs, and they then act to implement their promised programs.

Empirically, none of these three conditions is fully met in the United States. First, party leaders are not necessarily motivated to seek election primarily on the basis of policy programs. There is a basic conflict of goals between office seekers, who employ policy programs in their quest for power, and benefit seekers, who try to persuade these office seekers in their quest for particular programs. To the first group, policies are the instruments of electoral success; to the second they are the purpose of politics.[13]

Congress provides a good example. National legislators have three goals: winning election, gaining influence in the Senate or House of Representatives, and achieving good public policy. Of these goals, the most important to most legislators is winning election. Given such practices as committee specialization and individual perquisites, Congress is designed to serve these electoral interests rather than policy goals. Contrary to the expectations of the governing caucus model, "the enactment of party programs is electorally not very important to members. . . . What is important to each congressman, and vitally so, is that he be free to take positions that serve his interests."[14]

This electoral focus does not mean that legislators are simply unprincipled, selfish feeders at the public trough. It is only a recognition of the reality that election comes first in time—and therefore first in priority. A legislator cannot achieve any policy goals unless he or she first gets elected and stays in office long enough to accumulate influence within the legislature. Congress obviously does deal with policy but not as a party governing caucus. Rather, policy questions become relevant as part of the broader electoral needs of the representatives.

Policy programs are tied to elections in two different ways. First, politicians respond retrospectively. They interpret election results, often seeing their success as endorsements of their own programs and rejections of their opponents' programs.[15] They also try to read the tea leaves from other elections, interpreting the results, for example, as a mandate for lower taxes or evidence of a "new mood" among the public. Presidential popularity is particularly important since it has a direct effect on congressional elections; consequently, support for the president's program correlates closely with his standing among the electorate.[16]

Furthermore, politicians act prospectively, trying to anticipate the reactions and intentions of the electorate. Office seekers are often risk-taking entrepreneurs, attempting to find new "products" that will attract "buyers" in the electoral marketplace.[17] Enterprising legislators have developed such programs as Medicare, tax simplification, and abortion restrictions, achieving both policy change and electoral success.

Policy, then, is important to politicians, but this importance does not validate the governing caucus model. Rather than constituting a collective and coherent program, these policy initiatives are typically unconnected and distinct from one another. Politicians react to election returns individualistically, even idiosyncratically. The innovations they propose reflect their own interests and their particular election strategies, not a common party program. To recall Wilson's metaphor, the result is not a national broth but a stew whose ingredients follow no fixed recipe nor assure any nutritional balance.

The achievement of a common party program will depend on the parties' electoral situation. When their candidates face widespread competition, they may have an incentive for mutual aid and cooperation; by "hanging together," candidates may avoid the electoral death of "hanging separately." By achieving a common legislative program, they may be able to present a better record to their constituents. By sharing funds and services, they may be able to wage better campaigns.

The spread of party competition in the United States has promoted some increased cooperation within the parties. Among state parties, there is some tendency for party organizations to become more developed as they become more competitive.[18] On both the state and the national level, as legislators have felt more insecure, they have fostered collective electoral organizations.

Groups such as the Democratic Congressional Campaign Committee, the Republican Senatorial Campaign Committee, and political action committees run by legislative leaders have now become major sources of money and technical resources for their fellow partisans. Increased party cohesion on programs is also evident in Congress, where roll-call voting shows a higher degree of partisan unity than at any time since the end of World War II. The degree of party unity, however, is inherently limited by the basic electoral reality that congressional elections are held is disaggregated districts, where campaigns are centered on individual candidates, not on national parties.

Even when a party might develop a common program, the caucus model may not apply. To effect popular democratic control over policy, this model requires that the programs developed by the parties be distinct from one another, providing a choice for the electorate. Parties that are electorally sensitive, however, will not necessarily develop different programs, only popular programs. Indeed, when the wishes of the electorate are clear, party programs will be indentical rather than conflicting if the parties act rationally in their own self-interest.[19] Party differences will probably be the most distinct when there is no discernible popular preference for one or another policy. Paradoxically, the model therefore will be most evident when it is least relevant to democratic control.

These relationships between parties and the voters point to another set of problems in the caucus model: its unspoken assumptions about electoral behavior. For a governing caucus to achieve democratic legitimacy, it requires voter endorsement for its collective program. The extensive studies of voting (discussed further in chapter 7), however, show that a popular mandate is highly unlikely to exist.

A mandate first requires that voters make their choices on the basis of the programs advanced by parties. To be sure, there is considerable issue content to the popular vote, much more than was once believed. Although some votes are based only on traditional, issue-less loyalties and some are based on judgments of individual candidates, a substantial proportion is related to judgments of past and future programs advanced by the parties and their candidates. These judgments may not be specific in content, but they are still meaningful. As Fiorina puts it in discussing the issue basis of party loyalty, "By forming a long-term judgment about relatively stable leadership cadres that periodically compete for their votes, citizens appear to behave in a perfectly reasonable way."[20]

A mandate, however, implies not only voter concern for issues but a concern for the same issues and a majority endorsement of one party's position on these dominant issues. These conditions rarely if ever apply, for even when voters are concerned with issues, they are concerned with different issues. In 1988, for example, when asked to name the most important issue before the nation, only 12 percent agreed on the priority, the budget deficit, and even smaller proportions focused on other concerns.[21]

At other times, there has been more agreement on the priority issues, but still less than a majority. The most notable case of agreement among voters came in 1968, when public attention focused on the Vietnam War. Yet even in this time of national agony, only 43 percent, less than a majority, named the war as the priority issue of the election. In more normal times, an issue mandate is still less likely. Analyzing these patterns, Kelley concludes that even recent landslide presidential elections, except that of 1964, cannot be considered policy mandates.[22]

Mandates do not usually come from the voters but are defined by those voted into office. Yet definitions may vary, as those elected read the election returns differently. One representative may see her success as voter opposition to increased taxation while another interprets his victory as approval of legalized abortion. Politicans will be more likely to read the same meaning into elections when they share a common electoral fate, when they must hang together. Increased competition, however, does not assure this cooperation unless it also means increased competition for each individual candidate bearing the common party label. This condition does not apply in the contemporary Congress; incumbents are secure in their seats, with as many as 98 percent winning reelection.

Most of these legislators have little need either to gain support from the party or to provide much support to the party and its program. Even when not secure, legislators will not necessarily depend on their party but may actually find it more expedient to display their independence. Fenno's comment on the individualism of contemporary campaigning applies as much to the congressional party as to the national legislature: "Members of Congress run *for* Congress by running *against* Congress. . . . In the short run, everybody plays and nearly everybody wins. Yet the institution bleeds from 435 separate cuts. In the long run, therefore, somebody may lose."[23]

PARTIES IN GOVERNMENT

In its third operational aspect, the governing caucus model assumes that the party will implement its common program after receiving a voter mandate. In studying the effect of parties on government policy, analysts tend to apply the most exacting standards of the governing caucus model. They test whether parties take collective responsibility for a common program, for example, by examining legislative voting, gauging parties against an expected standard of total unanimity within each party and total difference between the parties. A more reasonable measure, however, might be whether parties show relative, rather than absolute, internal unity and external differences.

Judged on these criteria, parties clearly do affect legislative decisions. In congressional roll calls, partisanship is consistently the most important explanatory variable, and the impact of party on legislative behavior has increased in recent years. In 1990, half of the recorded votes found a majority of Democrats opposing a majority of Republicans, and the average legislator supported his or her party on more than three out of four instances of partisan roll calls.[24]

This difference is independent of the constituency pressures on members of Congress, as shown by an analysis of voting in both houses. Senators from the same state, sharing the same constituency but of different parties, vote quite differently. In the House, similarly, a change in party control of a seat also leads to a change in the representative's behavior. On average, a Democrat from the same area as a Republican will be forty-two points higher on a one hundred-point scale of liberalism.[25]

Parties differ from each other, but do they make a difference? Do they fight each other vigorously only over trivial issues, or can they actually affect the course of government? Government, after all, cannot control much of human life; indeed, in the modern technological and interdependent world, it can be argued that governments cannot even control their own economies.

Examining British public policy, Richard Rose doubts that either parties or government itself has much effect. Rather than adversarial conflict between the parties, he found considerable consensus between them (before the onset of the Thatcher government). Although parties did enact their election manifestos, these pledges involved only a small portion of the business of government. In the end, governmental action was not decided by elected politicians—or even by bureaucrats—but was inevitably determined by uncontrollable forces in the economy and in the world.[26] A similar argument has been made in regard to state government in the United States. The claim is that the level of governmental spending, a crucial index of party influence, depends not on political factors such as party competition but on such nonpolitical factors as the level of economic development.[27]

Parties cannot control their environment totally; still, they can have considerable effect. Party platforms provide one indicator. Although platforms are often denigrated as only empty rhetoric, closer analysis shows that the election manifestos of American parties are appropriate documents for a governing caucus. Although there is a minor proportion of windy clichés, most of the platforms either deal with the past records of the competing parties or propose particular public policies.

In their platforms, the parties do not simply imitate one another or cleave to the middle of the road, as would be expected if they followed purely winning strategies. Parties emphasize different issues, playing to different constituencies. Although they show bipartisan agreement on some issues, the degree of conflict is greater. By 1980, according to Monroe, the parties disagreed on nearly one-half of the significant issues in their platforms and agreed on only one-seventh.[28] Even more important, the parties actually carry through on their promises, fulfilling between two-thirds and three-fourths of their specific pledges. It may be significant, however, that the trend is toward lessened platform fulfillment, an indication of lower party strength in the United States.[29]

The more general effect of parties on government can be seen by examining patterns of governmental expenditures. In the American states, spending for such purposes as education is largely determined by the wealth of the state. When it comes to more politically controversial functions, such as welfare, party competition makes a difference. As the parties bid for votes, public spending increases.[30]

Even as they compete, the parties present and effect different programs. Among the states, a higher level of public spending in relevant policy areas occurs when Democrats rather than Republicans predominate.[31] Comparing nations, when parties of the Left are in power, government policy is directed more toward stimulating employment; governments headed by parties of the Right emphasize the control of inflation.[32] Economic realities restrict some choices, but politics makes a difference.

Parties also specialize, as they appeal to different constituencies. Two researchers compared the emphasis given to different policy topics by the two major American parties with national expenditures in these areas from 1948 to 1985. They found strong relationships, supporting a model of party as governing caucus, and conclude, "Party government in the U.S. works largely as mandate theories say it should, that is, responsively to electoral endorsements of party policy emphases.''[33]

Even with their substantial impact on policy, parties cannot fully meet the tests of the governing caucus model because of basic constitutional features of American government. Madison correctly predicted the workings of that government when he assured his readers that the new system of government would diminish "the influence of factious leaders" and would guarantee that "a rage for paper money, for an abolition of debts, for an equal division of property, or for any other improper or wicked project will be less apt to pervade the whole body of the Union than a particular member of it."[34] The same Constitution that prevented enactment of the programs Madison feared also limits the ability of a party caucus to enact other legislation, whether "improper or wicked" or necessary and good.

Federalism and the system of national checks and balances were deliberately—and successfully—designed to make it difficult to achieve a common party program. To effect basic changes in policy, a party must do more than win a single election, whatever its program and however clear a national mandate. It must win the presidency and both houses of Congress; it must also carry separate elections for the governors and legislatures of the states. Even with these victories, it cannot be certain of the endorsement of judges or of the cooperation of administrators. Gaining control of these branches of government would require sustained success over a long period of time, to enable the party to place its loyalists throughout the judiciary and the bureaucracy.

The barriers faced by a governing caucus are particularly high on questions of foreign policy, the most vital issues facing the United States or any nation. This type of political party is legitimated by its majority support, but that warrant is insufficient for a governing party on these issues. Vital decisions affecting war and peace require a broader public consensus, and the Constitution adds the institutional necessity that the Senate ratify treaties by a two-thirds vote.

Woodrow Wilson's own history illustrates the problem. When Wilson brought the League of Nations Treaty to the Senate after World War I, he attempted to implement the theory of party as a governing caucus. At first, Wilson took a nonpartisan approach, negotiating with Republican senators and seeking public support through a nationwide speaking tour. Then, as the issue moved to resolution, Wilson acted in keeping with his concept of the political party. He pressed for party loyalty in the Senate vote and saw the forthcoming election as the opportunity to achieve a popular mandate for himself and for his party program. Writing to the Democrats' annual Jackson Day dinner, Wilson attempted to frame the 1920 election as "a great and solemn referendum, a referendum on the part the United States is to play in completing the settlements of the war."

Neither effort succeeded. The party split in the Senate and, as twenty Democrats followed Wilson's leadership and refused to compromise, the treaty was defeated by seven votes. The electorate, moreover, was not offered a clear choice in the presidential contest and did not vote primarily on the issue of the League of Nations. Wilson was faithful to his own theory of political parties. The reality demonstrated in this critical case, however, was that the party could not hold together, that voters would not provide a simple mandate, and that the institutions of American government were inhospitable to party rule. In the end, by following theory to its ultimate conclusion, the president "spelled disaster for ratification of the Treaty in any form. Wilson committed the supreme error of converting what had really not been a partisan issue, except in the parliamentary sense, into a hostage of party loyalty and politics."[35]

Party as governing caucus always has been problematic in the United States, and in contemporary times the difficulties have increased. The two-party system, potentially an instrument of majority rule, has been virtually transformed into a new separation of powers, as Republicans have come to dominate presidential elections (losing convincingly only once since the era of Franklin Roosevelt) and Democrats have come to dominate congressional elections (losing control of the House for only two years since 1948).

With these electoral developments, American government has become increasingly subject to institutional deadlock. "As each party has strengthened the institutions it commands," Ginsberg and Shefter argue, "the constitutional separation of powers has been transformed into a system of dual sovereignty." The consequences include the inability of the government to achieve "political closure" and the weakening of the nation's administrative capabilities, making vital national issues difficult to resolve.[36] Even when those problems are overcome, their resolution typically occurs outside of the normal political processes, through administrative and judicial decisions or through nonpartisan or bipartisan commissions. Their mechanisms provide scant support for the model of party as governing caucus.

PARTY AS CAUSE ADVOCATE

The governing caucus is an elite party, but it has a counterpart among mass parties, the party as cause advocate. This party is also concerned primarily with collective issues, and its appeal is the policy rewards it offers to its adherents. Attention focuses on enlisting popular endorsement of these policies, however, rather than on elite programs.

Ostrogorski argues for such parties. After condemning the normal organizations of his day, he urged parties that would have only mass, external relationships:

> Party as a general contractor for the numerous and varied problems present and to come, awaiting solution, would give place to special organizations, limited to particular objects. It would cease to be a medley of groups and individuals united by a fictitious agreement, and would constitute an association, the homogeneity of which would be ensured by its single aim. Party holding its members, once they have joined it, in a vice-like grasp would give place to combinations forming and reforming spontaneously, according to the changing problems of life and the play of opinion.[37]

Party as cause advocate already exists, to some extent. Even the major American parties can sometimes be described this way, for their leaders often define their roles as advocates of programs rather than as simply followers of public opinion and seekers after office.[38] Splinter parties within the major parties are also often of this variety, constituting efforts "to win the party to more complete commitment to their views."[39] Such diverse dissidents as Van Buren's 1848 Free Soilers, the southern Democratic "Dixiecrats" of 1948, the "Peace and Freedom" offshoot of liberal Democrats in the 1970s, and John Anderson's Independent movement in 1980 were attempts to influence the policy programs of their own parties, rather than genuine efforts to build new, permanent parties.

Cause advocates face even more barriers to success than those encountered in a governing caucus party. Because of the restricted range of their policy concerns, they are less likely to be able to build majority coalitions. If it is difficult to obtain a mandate from the electorate on even large and general issues, it is still more difficult on the specific issues of concern to cause groups.

Furthermore, the electorate's concerns change, sometimes rapidly. A party with a more general outlook may be able to adapt to these changes, incorporating new issues within its old framework or even shifting to new concerns, but a party based on a particular issue always risks becoming archaic. The Prohibition party provides an example. For fifty years, the issue of the regulation of alcohol was of great importance in American politics and eventually brought amendment of the Constitution. Today, after that "great experiment" has failed, the Prohibitionists continue to advocate their cause, but their party is completely dry.[40]

THE GOVERNING CAUCUS AND DEMOCRACY

The problems of the party as governing caucus go beyond the considerable practical hurdles it faces in the United States; it also has theoretical problems in relating party to democratic governance. The governing caucus model attempts to provide democratic legitimacy for a political party that involves very limited democratic participation. Essentially, the model focuses on leadership, which invites popular participation only to approve its program in a limited election and then expects the populace to do nothing more than applaud that leadership.

Burke made clear the distinction between leaders and followers in his famous speech to his electorate in Bristol. Voters could choose their representative, but they must defer to his superior judgment. Constituents could legitimately demand attention from their legislator, "but his unbiased opinion, his mature judgment, his enlightened conscience, he ought not to sacrifice to you, to any man, or to any set of men living, . . . [for] government and legislation are matters of reason and judgment, and not of inclination."[41]

Wilson similarly emphasized this central idea, consistently seeking means "to provide for concentrated leadership and power inside the official government structure."[42] Effective democratic government, he argued, requires "coordinated power for leaders" and simplification for the electorate: "We must decrease the number and complexity of the things the voter is called upon to do; concentrate his attention upon a few men whom he can make responsible, a few objects upon which he can easily center his purpose; make parties his instruments and not his masters by an utter simplification of the things he is expected to do."[43]

Leaders are informed; voters are fallible. Burke aristocratically feared that passions would distort popular judgment, as evidenced both by English opposition to the American Revolution and French support for their revolutionary Reign of Terror. Wilson was more confident that mass opinion, if it were properly led, could achieve "a new and cordial and easily attained understanding between those who govern and those who are governed."[44] To both men, the relationship was not one between equal participants in a democratic polity; it was more akin to that of a teacher of passive but educable students. Burke engaged in political education as much as Wilson, who indeed did lecture, to his students and to his national constituency. Their classroom was not an example of progressive "learning by doing" but one in which students absorbed wisdom from their instructor. If dissatisfied, the students did not engage in argument but simply left the room to find a more acceptable teacher.

In the democracy of the governing caucus, leadership is responsible because it can be dismissed collectively by an electorate dissatisfied with its programs. That accessibility is limited, however. Because responsibility is collective, few direct ties exist between an individual leader and an individual voter; there is no person to deal directly with a voter's unique needs, in the manner of a machine precinct leader. Relying largely on elections to control leaders, the governing caucus model provides sparse means for control between elections or on matters that do not arise in elections or on the vital details of public policies that go undefined in elections.

The emphasis on leadership stilts democracy, limiting it by restricting involvement in the development of party programs. Those in the governing caucus develop programs—others only approve or disapprove. Such participation is shallow, but efforts to deepen popular participation create other problems.

In its call for strengthened parties, the 1950 Committee on Political Parties advocated both strong and centralized leadership and extensive popular participation in the writing of enforceable party programs. Adopting both goals, however, does not resolve the tensions between them. There is no logical assurance that leaders and other party members will share the same programmatic goals, unless we wrongly assume that all party memberships are based on full knowledge and approval of leadership policies. In fact, the evidence consistently refutes this assumption. Repeated studies have shown that Democratic party leaders are considerably more liberal and Republicans considerably more conservative than their rank-and-file memberships.[45] For example, in 1988, 51 percent of Democratic party convention delegates favored federal funding of abortions, but Democratic voters opposed it by nearly a two-to-one margin; among Republican convention delegates, 51 percent opposed the Equal Rights Amendment, but Republican voters favored the amendment by a seven-to-one margin.[46]

Moreover, ordinary party loyalists, in general, tend to be like one another, but the leaders of their parties tend to disagree. This finding implies that if rank-and-file members participated fully in the formulation of party programs, these programs would be more similar to each other and would offer less choice to the general electorate. The result is a democratic paradox: full popular involvement in developing policy would translate into less meaningful popular choice; conversely, leadership domination over policy development would provide more meaningful choice.

Democracy is further stilted in the governing caucus model because that model relies heavily on programmatic appeals. Politics, after all, is a human relationship, involving affection as well as intellect. Government depends on the character of its leaders as well as on their arguments; voters, in choosing leaders, properly invoke their passions as well as their interests. In a vibrant democracy, parties will accept and channel these emotions, recognizing that loyalties to parties, and their voter support, go beyond reasoned appeals.

The governing caucus, however, is too much a matter of cold reasoning, as illustrated in the lives of its most prominent advocates. When Burke broke with his party over the French Revolution, he also felt it necessary to deny his emotions and loyalties. Policy disagreement inevitably meant personal estrangement: "There was a loss of friends—he knew the price of his conduct . . . their friendship was at an end."[47] When Wilson saw the League of Nations repudiated by members of his party and the voters, he became embittered and felt abandoned.

Relying too much on their intellectual appeal, these brilliant men still lacked some essential traits of democratic leaders. As Max Weber taught, "Politics is a strong and slow boring of hard boards. It takes both passion and perspective. . . . Only he has the calling for politics who is sure that he shall not crumble when the world from his point of view is too stupid or too base for what he wants to offer."[48] Democracy requires more than a governing caucus; it needs parties that recognize and foster both personal passion and ideological perspective.

FOUR

COMMON PASSIONS: PARTY AS IDEOLOGICAL COMMUNITY AND SOCIAL MOVEMENT

We few, we happy few, we band of brothers . . .
—*William Shakespeare*, Henry V

We stand at Armageddon and we battle for the Lord.
—*Theodore Roosevelt, 1912*

The organization must consist chiefly of persons
engaged in revolution as a profession.
—*V. I. Lenin*, What Is to Be Done?

A political party may have broader goals beyond electoral victory and thus expect more of its members. As ideological communities and as social movements, parties use the expressive mode and pursue collective goals, but they differ in their focus. Parties as ideological communities are likely to be relatively closed or elite groups, like the governing caucus. In contrast, social movements mobilize mass participation and are readily accessible to mass influence.

In one or the other form, these models are often seen as the ideal political party, one that joins its members in a common effort to achieve social reconstruction. Politics becomes a crusade for justice rather than a mean chase for personal advantage. Robert Michels had hoped that the Socialist party would fulfill this ideal.

Americans, too, have been inspired by this ideal, typically when they have been involved in expressive third parties. In the United States, these parties evidence characteristics both of the elite-oriented ideological community and of the mass-oriented social movement. Important examples include the antislavery Free Soil party of antebellum days, the Populist protesters against capitalist development at the end of the nineteenth century, and the fervent legions supporting Theodore Roosevelt's Progressive campaign in 1912. These parties have been important participants in the democratic contests of the United States.

THE LENINIST PARTY

To better understand the character of such parties, however, we first turn to a different context and a different writer: Vladimir Lenin, the founder of the nondemocratic Russian Communist party and the leader of the party's revolutionary creation of the Soviet Union. Lenin's thought was shaped in the context of Tsarist Russia, an authoritarian, centralized regime with little concern for individual freedom. His model of a political party reflects these characteristics. His Social Democratic (later Bolshevik and Communist) party was also authoritarian and centralized and totally dominated the lives of its members. Through this party, he sought—and achieved—a collective program for the total replacement of the tsarist regime.

The Leninist party is an elite party, confined to a small group of selected and dedicated members, totally committed and totally controlled. Only through such means, Lenin argued, can the party achieve its true goal: revolution. The party must not only lead the revolution, it must call it into being, for insurrections are made, not born.

The party is to be the "vanguard of the revolution," raising the working-class above its usual, paltry concerns for limited economic improvements in wages and hours. "This consciousness among workers," Lenin insisted, "could only be brought to them from without. The history of all countries shows that the working class, exclusively by its own effort, is able to develop only trade-union consciousness."[1]

The vanguard party's role is important—for without it the revolution can never take place—but it is also exacting, requiring intense training and discipline. The party will consist of professional revolutionaries, persons who "recognize its program and support the party both materially and by personal participation."[2] Seeking the overthrow of the government requires a structured, clandestine party, for only then can success be guaranteed against attacks by the government. Secrecy is particularly important to the party, so much so that "all the other conditions (number and selection of members, functions, etc.) must all be subordinated to it. . . . 'Broad democracy' in party organization, amidst the gloom of autocracy and the domination of the gendarmes, is nothing more than a useless and harmful toy."[3]

The party dominates the lives of its members. Invoking the imagery of wartime comradeship, Lenin praises his elite:

We are marching in a compact group along a precipitous and difficult path, firmly holding each other by the hand. We are surrounded on all sides by enemies, and are under their almost constant fire. We have combined voluntarily, especially for the purpose of fighting the enemy and not to retreat into the adjacent marsh, the inhabitants of which, right from the very outset, have reproached us with having separated ourselves into an exclusive group, and with having chosen the path of struggle instead of the path of conciliation.[4]

Lenin scorns the democratic principle of "freedom of criticism" as mere self-defeating opportunism, "the freedom to convert Social-Democracy into a democratic reformist party, the freedom to introduce bourgeois ideas and bourgeois elements into Socialism." Instead of debate within the party, he insists on adherence to a common revolutionary ideology, for "the role of vanguard can be fulfilled only by a party that is guided by an advanced theory."[5]

Beyond an encompassing theory, the Leninist party requires "iron discipline" to combat "that petty-bourgeois diffusiveness, instability, [and] incapacity for sustained effort, unity and organized action, which, if indulged in, must inevitably destroy every proletarian revolution."[6] Discipline is to be hierarchical and strictly enforced by a central organization, which is to make all major decisions for the party.

Lenin unapologetically demands centralized authority: "The organization principle of revolutionary Social Democracy . . . strives to proceed from the top downwards, insisting on the extension of the rights and authority of the center over the parts."[7] Implementation of this disciplinary code is illustrated in factories, where every party worker "must regard himself as an agent of the committee, obliged to subordinate himself to the orders of the committee and to adhere to all the 'laws and customs' of that 'army on active service' which he has joined and which in time of war he has no right to abandon without the consent of his superior."[8]

Like all parties, Lenin's elite organization seeks mass support, but it does so through a separate popular base. "The secret apparatus of the party must be preserved. But at the same time . . . in addition to the secret apparatus it is absolutely necessary to create many new, public and semipublic party organizations."[9] These broader organizations will be guided by the elite party beyond their immediate objectives toward support of the collective goals.

To illustrate, industrial workers must be deliberately taught to generalize

the class struggle: "Working class consciousness cannot be genuinely political consciousness unless the workers are trained to respond to all cases of
tyranny, oppression, violence and abuse, no matter what class is affected."[10]
That training comes through the actions of the inner party: "They should
go into the most common inns, penetrate into the unions, societies and
casual meetings where the common people gather, and talk to the people,
not in scientific (and not in very parliamentary) language . . . but every-
where arouse the thoughts of the masses and draw them into the struggle."[11]

Through these activities, the goal of the Leninist party remains a total
social transformation through the revolution of the working class. In his
only direct repudiation of Marx, Lenin insists that this transformation can
take place only through violence, even in the ostensibly democratic nations.
"Both England and America, the greatest and last representatives of Anglo-
Saxon 'Liberty' in the sense of the absence of militarism and bureaucracy,
have today plunged headlong into the all-European, dirty, bloody morass
of military bureaucratic institutions to which everything is subordinated and
which trample everything under foot."[12]

AMERICAN SOCIAL MOVEMENTS

The Leninist party is an extreme example of the concept of the political
party as an ideological community. Some of the same characteristics are
evident among certain American party organizations, especially the recurrent social movements represented by "third," or minority, parties.

These parties are similar to the Leninist party in their emphasis on collective goals and in their expressive character, yet they are critically different in their attitude toward democracy. Leninism disparages democracy,
but American third parties have supported and attempted to extend it. This
vital difference is also evident within the parties. The Leninist party champions elite control; the American party typically will urge more membership participation within the party and fuller mass participation in politics
generally.

Particularly relevant are the Populist and the Progressive parties of the
late nineteenth and early twentieth centuries. The Populist party developed
in the last two decades of the nineteenth century, reacting to the economic
disadvantages imposed on small farmers, who faced a devastating combination of depressed crop prices, a tight money supply, dependence on

exploitative railroads and suppliers, and high prices for industrial goods protected by high tariffs. In reaction to these conditions, aggrieved farmers created the Agrarian Alliance, with suballiances forming in local communities throughout the Midwest and the South. To meet farmers' needs, the alliance developed economic measures, such as marketing and credit cooperatives, and political programs, such as the use of paper money and silver to inflate the currency.

Most important, argues the leading analyst of the movement, the alliance developed an expressive "movement culture":

> This culture involved more than just the bulking of cotton. It extended to frequent Alliance meetings to plan the mass sales — meetings where the whole family came, where the twilight suppers were, in the early days, laid out for ten or twenty members of the suballiance, or for hundreds at a county Alliance meeting, but which soon grew into vast spectacles; long trains of wagons, emblazoned with suballiance banners, stretching literally for miles, trekking to enormous encampments where five, ten, and twenty thousand men and women listened intently to the plans of their Alliance and talked among themselves about these plans.
>
> The movement culture would develop its own mechanism of recruitment (the large-scale credit cooperative), its own theoretical analysis (the Greenback interpretation of the American version of finance capitalism), its own solution (the sub-treasury land and loan system), its own symbols of politics (the Alliance "Demands" and the Omaha Platform), and its own political institution (the People's Party). Grounded in a common experience, nurtured by years of experimentation and self-education, it produced a party, a platform, a specific new democratic ideology, and a pathbreaking political agenda for the American nation. But none of these things were the essence of Populism. At bottom, Populism was, quite simply, an expression of self-respect. It was not an individual trait, but a collective one, surfacing as the shared hope of millions organized by the Alliance into its cooperative crusade. This individual and collective striving generated the movement culture that was Populism.[13]

Eventually, the protest movement turned to politics. Formulating an extensive program for social change in the United States, the People's Party in its 1892 Omaha platform called for nationalization of the railroads, telegraph and telephone systems, a graduated income tax, restrictions of land ownership by corporations, and a national paper currency. The Populists presented themselves as speakers for the working class. In language better known in the writings of Marx and Lenin, they declared, "Wealth belongs to him who creates it, and every dollar taken from industry without an equivalent is robbery. 'If any will not work, neither shall he eat.' "

Radical as these specific proposals were for the time, the more striking characteristic of the Populist platform was its comprehensive, collective, and moralistic character. The preamble to the platform depicted a nation requiring not simply new programs but fundamental redemption:

> We meet in the midst of a nation brought to the verge of moral, political, and material ruin. Corruption dominates the ballot-box, the Legislatures, the Congress, and touches even the ermine of the bench. The people are demoralized. . . . The newspapers are largely subsidized or muzzled, public opinion silenced, business prostrated, homes covered with mortgages, labor impoverished, and the land concentrating in the hand of capitalists. . . . The fruits of the toil of millions are boldly stolen to build up colossal fortunes for a few, unprecedented in the history of mankind. . . . From the same prolific womb of governmental injustice we breed the two great classes—tramps and millionaires.
>
> We declare that this Republic can only endure as a free government while built upon the love of the whole people for each other and for the nation; that it cannot be pinned together by bayonets; and that the civil war is over and that every passion and resentment which grew out of it must die with it, and that we must be in fact, as we are in name, one united brotherhood of freemen.[14]

The Populists were a true community, but in contrast to Lenin's party, it was built on a mass, not an elite, base. It pursued an ideological program, but the full character of populism went beyond program to a deeply personal, expressive experience. "The cooperative ethos was the animating spirit of the popular movement they created—it literally gave hundreds of thousands of impoverished people what Martin Luther King would later call a 'sense of somebodiness.' "[15] It was a "passionate moment in American history," resulting in "the most massive organizing drive by any citizen institution of nineteenth-century America. ... The Alliance's five-year campaign carried lecturers into forty-three states and territories and touched two million American farm families."[16]

The People's Party crested in 1892 when it won close to one-tenth of the national vote for president and carried five states. In 1896, its most prominent issue, the unlimited coinage of silver to increase the money supply, was co-opted by the Democrats, led by William Jennings Bryan. The Populists then faced a critical decision, whether to endorse Bryan to further this one goal or to maintain their independence and their fuller and more radical program. The choice was not only about political strategy; it was also a choice of whether to maintain the model of a political party as an ideological community.

> At bottom, the third party's internal struggle was a contest between a cooperating group of political office-seekers on the one hand and the Populist movement on the other. The politicians had short-run objectives—winning the next election. In contrast, the agrarian movement, both as shaped by the Alliance organizers who had recruited the party's mass base of partisans and as shaped by the recruits themselves, had long-term goals, fashioned during the years of cooperative struggle and expressed politically in the planks of the Omaha Platform. While the movement itself had a mass following, the only popular support that the office-seekers could muster within the third party itself was centered in those regions of the country which the cooperative crusade had never been able to penetrate successfully. . . . In general, therefore, the contest between Populism and its shadow form in 1896 arrayed the politics of a people's movement against conventional electoral politics.[17]

In this instance, conventional politics won. While maintaining most of its previous positions, the People's Party declared the currency question "the great and pressing issue of the pending campaign." On this ground it downplayed its radicalism, endorsed Bryan for president, and quickly passed from the political scene. The Populists did have a long-term influence, moving the Democrats toward the left of the economic spectrum, but the cost of that influence was the party's death.

Another collective community in American politics was the Progressive party of 1912, led by former president Theodore Roosevelt. Like the Popu-

lists, this third party was a reaction to the development of industrial capitalism in the United States. Its focus, however, was different, emphasizing
not the problems of agriculture but the needs of a national, manufacturing,
and increasingly urban economy.

The affective fervor of the Progressives made it virtually a religious
movement. As one of its leaders described the party's national convention:

> The Progressive party, under Roosevelt, was going to free the United
> States not only from political and economic but from spiritual night.
> It was to rout Taft's Republican hosts, but this was merely a prelude
> to routing all the hosts of darkness. ... In the innocence of our hearts
> we believed that all that was required to reach the holy city of our
> dreams was to huddle ourselves and our aspirations under one great
> umbrella and to advance, saint and sinner, patriot and politician, with
> arms entwined and voices raised in song. ... Through them all a sort
> of rage for righteousness presently began to surge. Soon the conven-
> tion was keyed to the pitch of crusade. A religious fervor took pos-
> session of it. "Onward Christian Soldiers" and the "Doxology"
> tolled in the Coliseum as solemnly as in a cathedral.[18]

The Progressives matched this fervor by an extensive program of social
reform, including inheritance and income taxation, urban depopulation,
national health care, national regulation of corporations, and agricultural
cooperatives. More important than any specific proposals was its belief in
a discoverable, common public good beyond particular interests. "To this
end the party appeals to the Nation on the broadest possible basis; it attacks
no class; it obliterates sectionalism; it refuses to recognize sex distinction
in the rights of citizenship. It is the clean, free instrument of all the people —
of honest business, big and little; of the farmer and the wage-earner; of
every liberty-loving man and woman."[19]

The movement sought a collective goal, the moral no less than the economic reform of the nation. For this grand end, grand means were needed.
The core of the Progressive program was not so much the specifics of
industrial legislation but major changes in political procedures, such as the
direct primary, initiative, campaign finance, and even popular referenda
on court decisions. Social progress would be gained "by the exposure of
evils through the spreading of information and the exhortation of the citi-

zenry; by using the possibilities inherent in the ballot to find new and vigorous popular leaders; in short, by a revivification of democracy."[20]

Underlying the emphasis on political reform were two other quite different beliefs in collective action. The first was the religious spirit that animated progressivism, "an all-consuming urge to purge the world of sin. ... [They] believed it was their Christian duty to right the wrongs created by the processes of industrialization." Joined to this evangelical fervor was a more modern belief in objective scientific knowledge, a new faith "that knowledge of natural laws would make it possible to devise and apply solutions to improve the human condition."[21]

The new party made a strong debut in presidential politics, coming in second in the election of 1912 with 27 percent of the vote and carrying six states with eighty-eight electoral votes. As with the Populists, however, the demands of more practical politics defeated the ideological appeal. As World War I approached America, Roosevelt deserted the Progressives to reunite the Republican party. The Progressive party itself had submerged by the 1916 election; still, it made a strong impact on the administration of Wilson, as a revived party in 1924, and as a continuing attitude toward politics and parties.

IDEOLOGY AND PARTIES

Party as an ideological community is not only a theoretical model; it has also been tested by experience. At first glance, the model would seem deficient. The Leninist party achieved apparent great success, not only in its revolution against tsarist Russia but in the extension of Communist rule to China and Eastern Europe. Yet in longer historical perspective, that success now seems hollow, as the citizens of Eastern Europe have decisively rejected Communist regimes in free elections and Chinese dissent has been forcibly repressed. Leninism has been repudiated even in its historical heartland, as the Soviet Union has disappeared, replaced by newly independent and decidedly non-Communist states.

Behind these failures of Communist parties is a change in their character, their transformation from ideological communities to other forms, to governing caucuses or bureaucratic organizations. Milovan Djilas used Marxist theory itself to explain the emergence of a "new class" from the Communist party, "made up of those who have special privileges and economic preference because of the administrative monopoly they hold." Lenin's ideological community had become a materialistic oligarchy:

> Membership in the Communist Party before the Revolution meant sacrifice. Being a professional revolutionary was one of the highest honors. Now that the party has consolidated its power, party membership means that one belongs to a privileged class. And at the core of the party are the all-powerful exploiters and masters.[22]

The loss of vigorous ideological commitment is a more general problem of political parties, not simply the manifestation of a fatal flaw in communism. Michels had deplored this transformation of the German Social Democrats, and his theory would predict similar decay among similar parties. The same pattern is evident among American third-party movements, whose histories are patterned stories of rapid political rises and even more rapid declines. The Populists, for example, made an impressive start in presidential politics in 1892, voluntarily subordinated their program to the Democrats in 1896, and declined to insignificance by the end of the century.

These patterns may be rooted in human psychology. Parties as ideological communities demand much from their members, emotionally as well as intellectually. It is certainly difficult for people to maintain a long-term commitment to abstract ideologies rather than to personal interests, just as it is difficult to maintain for long the expressive fervor of these parties. After a time, narrower, more personal, more immediate, and calmer attitudes and allegiances come to dominate. Romantic ardor gives way to reflective affection or even to calculation.

To explain the transformation of parties structured as ideological communities, we need to examine the structure of incentives provided by organizations generally, including parties. These incentives can be classified along two dimensions. The first dimension is their tangible or intangible nature. On this dimension, incentives may be material and tangible, such as a patronage job, or psychological and intangible, such as representation of ethnic groups on a party's ticket. The second dimension is the divisible or collective nature of the incentive. A divisible incentive, such as a party-leadership position, can be given as a reward to some people and denied as a punishment to others. A collective benefit, such as the party's governmental program, is inherently available to all persons in the organization, regardless of their individual efforts or merit.

In an ideological community, leaders constantly face the problem of inducing effort toward the achievement of "collective goods," those benefits that accrue to persons with or without their individual effort. If the party wins an election, for example, all members will share in the psychological elation and perhaps reap some satisfaction from new public policies, regardless of their personal involvement. There is a constant temptation in these circumstances for members, busy with their own lives, to slacken their own efforts, to "let George do it."[23] Seeking to avoid the decay of ideological fervor, Leninist parties engage in periodic purges, just as religious movements rekindle their energies through evangelical revivals.

Given these problems, analysts have been skeptical of the role of ideological incentives in American political parties, doubting either the existence or the workability of these incentives. Considerable scholarship now exists, however, to indicate that ideology is an important factor within American parties. Such incentives may be necessary under modern conditions in the United States; despite some problems, the parties seem able to endure under these conditions.

The traditional view of American parties has been that they are without

> ideological or programmatic commitment in both the front and rear ranks. . . . They are vast, gaudy, friendly umbrellas under which all Americans, whoever and whatever and however-minded they may be, are invited to stand for the sake of being counted in the next election. . . . The parties, moderate and tolerant and self-contradictory to a fault, are interested in the votes of men, not in their principles, and they care not at all whether the votes they gather are bestowed with passion or indifference—so long as they are bestowed and counted.

Moreover, in this view, the lack of party principle is desirable. In their very lack of principle, "the parties have been the peacemakers of the American community, the unwitting but forceful suppressors of the 'civil war potential' we carry always in the bowels of our diverse nation."[24]

In the 1960s American politics became more conflictful, and the major parties came under the increased influence of ideological activists. This development induced two different criticisms. The first was itself ideological, particularly directed toward the enhanced role of left-leaning liberals in the Democratic party. One neoconservative pointedly criticized what she saw as the "contemptuous elite" of the anti–Vietnam War movement:

"There was contempt for the nineteen-year-old boys who were carrying guns in the war or in the Guard. It was understood that they were uneducated, and somewhat crude. There was contempt for America."[25] The second critique, more relevant here, was that ideological parties, whether Left or Right, would be less effective. If each of the parties presented a cohesive appeal, conflict would increase between them, threatening the stability of the overall political system. If only one party were ideological, its narrowed base would doom it to defeat.

An inherent tension exists between the goals of winning elections and achieving preferred public policy, paralleled by conflict between professional party leaders and ideological purists:

> What professional party leaders ordinarily care about most is getting their candidates into office and keeping them there. Other considerations are usually secondary. . . . When parties are purist, activists control candidates. The purpose of such parties is to espouse policies of which party activists approve. If they do that and win, so much the better for them; if the price of purism is defeat, so much the worse for the candidate. If a choice has to be made by purist activists, purism outside office is better than power in government.[26]

Examining ideological local Democratic parties—which he disdained as "amateurs"—James Wilson found them handicapped. Seeking the participation of their members inevitably and fatally creates "the need of amateur leaders continually to commit themselves on issues and to follow the logic of their position beyond the point where it can any longer be the basis for the formulation of public policy." These parties are led to extreme and unpopular positions, to refusals to compromise, to the rejection of coalitions with potential allies, and then inevitably to electoral defeats and the frustration of their own policy goals.[27]

Despite these critiques, accumulated research over the past three decades reveals a very different picture of American parties. Even in the calmer times of the 1950s, national convention delegates of the major parties were quite distinct from each other ideologically. Republicans were clearly conservative and Democrats leaned toward liberalism. Similarities in ideology did exist, but not among the party leaders; rather, the similarities existed among the mass electorate, where Republican and Democratic voters shared many beliefs.[28]

This early evidence has been confirmed repeatedly. Among their leaderships, American parties, contrary to conventional wisdom, often are "advocacy parties." The parties do not repress ideological conflicts among the electorate; on the contrary, they muffle their own beliefs to win the support of a less ideological electorate.

The ideological distinctiveness of the parties has been demonstrated at local, state, and national levels. A large survey of state convention delegates in eleven diverse states invariably showed "the consistent liberalism of the Democrats and the consistent conservatism of the Republicans." Even more striking are comparisons across states. Democrats were liberal not only in comparison to their party counterparts in the same state but were ideologically akin throughout the nation. Even the most conservative Democrats in any state were still more liberal than the most liberal Republicans in any state.[29]

Similar conclusions follow from a long-term study of party activists attending national party conventions over the past two decades. In 1980, for example, only an insignificant 2 percent of Republicans called themselves liberals, closely matched by the 6 percent of Democrats who called themselves conservatives. Over time, the general tendency has been for the differences between these party leaderships to increase over a wide range of issues, including foreign and defense policy, the environment, abortion, and national economic and welfare programs.[30]

Although the parties have become more ideological, they are not necessarily less effective. Party activists hold their principles strongly but also support their party. There is a "strong commitment to party among all cadres of contemporary party elites—and certainly little indication of the loss of party regularity assumed by many political scientists. Judged in this light, the postreform party system is in robust health."[31] With longer experience, activists are less likely to insist on "standing firm for position even if it means resigning from the party" and show increasingly strong commitment to the party. The so-called amateurs' "enthusiasm for ideological purity at the expense of party was apparently short-lived."[32]

A similar preference is seen among state-party activists when they must choose between electoral success and ideological purity. Being human, partisans like to believe they can have it both ways and that the candidates closer to their favored program are also preferred by the voters. When forced to make a choice, however, party activists of all ideological persuasions choose electability over purity.[33] Ideology does not necessarily doom parties to failure if it is balanced by electoral pragmatism.

Ideological incentives do cause problems. Persons recruited into a political party for ideological reasons are apt to be unrepresentative, either of the voters in general or even of the party's own mass base. Particularly in contemporary parties of the Left, an ideological emphasis is more likely to result in domination of the party by middle-class intellectuals than by manual workers.[34] Furthermore, this emphasis may harm the party by restricting the maneuverability of party leaders in choosing optimal policy positions in their search for votes.[35]

At the same time, ideological incentives offer some advantages for a party, even in a limited utilitarian sense. They provide, at the least, a basis for attracting members. "A party must have a principle; for though it may live without a principle for years, it loses its usefulness, and finds its enlisted men, little by little, deserting." Ideology is therefore an important element in the quest for electoral victory, making a party without principles "unfortunate, not vicious."[36] Furthermore, ideological incentives have particular merits. Because ideology is collective, not individual, party leaders do not necessarily disappoint some members when they reward others, as they inevitably do with divisible rewards. Because ideology is intangible, it is economically cheap and may not even need to be achieved to be effective. A promise of a job must be redeemed; the promise of a better society can be reiterated regularly and still inspire the members' devotion.

Although American parties are certainly not ideological communities, these incentives are becoming increasingly important to them. A significant transformation in contemporary political parties is evidenced in a greater emphasis on public goods, as ideology becomes a more common incentive for party activity. Parties still provide material rewards, but these are no longer commonly those of patronage or office. Rather, material rewards are given to those outside the parties, such as financial contributors, or to those technical experts who provide services inside the party organization.

Policy causes motivate many of the individual contributors to the parties as well as some political action committees. Their ideological commitments stimulate the financial contributions that in turn pay for advertising, polling, campaigning experts, and policy analysts. Some contributors to the parties, of course, hope to be nominated as a foreign ambassador or to gain favor for their special legislative interest. A large proportion, however, contribute to Democrats or Republicans to advance their notion of the public good, to promote not their own interests but those of unborn fetuses or the homeless poor.

Ideological incentives are also needed to stimulate person-to-person campaigning. Neither the material nor the ethnic appeals of the traditional machine will sustain political parties at the local level. There, the passionate advocates of religious orthodoxy or nuclear disarmament are more likely to be knocking on doors than the fabled but absent party precinct captains. Parties no longer can choose between a professional emphasis on electoral success and an "amateur" emphasis on ideological purism. Both are needed today if either is to be achieved.

IDEOLOGY AND DEMOCRACY

The model of a political party as an ideological community is attractive. It combines such laudable objectives as a devotion to principle, a commitment to others, and a search for the public good. In reading the history of the Populists, for example, we inveitably feel sympathy for their distressed constituents and admiration for their efforts toward social justice and broadened participation.

Yet Lenin also intrudes. The ideological party, in its Communist variety, has achieved not social justice but repression, not equality but a domineering bureaucracy. Beyond the historical connection between Leninist party doctrine and Leninist authoritarian practice, there also is a possible logical connection. The very fervor and collective focus of this model may also induce a disregard for individual interests and liberties.

In the model of an ideological community, the party relies primarily on intangible and collective incentives. Persons will give their time, energy, even their lives to the party, not for personal and material gain but in order to serve the larger cause and to express social solidarity with their party brothers and sisters. To be sure, such human idealism is real and recurrent, but it is an uncertain base for continued political action. Leaders must constantly inspire their followers, working against the common tendencies of self-interest, parochialism, "trade-union consciousness," or simple fatigue.

An ideological party always faces the possibility that it will lose its zeal, that its followers will no longer stand at Armageddon but stray into more comfortable green pastures. A common response in such organizations is to develop alternative and more personal incentives. If commitment to the party program flags, offer the members group discounts on airline fares; if solidarity with the working class weakens, create workers' recreational clubs. Such techniques may maintain the level of membership but at the cost of ideological concern. As Michels unhappily observes: "A bowling club remains a bowling club even if it assumes the pompous name of 'Sons of Freedom Bowling Club.' "[37]

Other means serve to maintain ideological zeal. One is to limit participation to those who remain true to the faith, a technique well developed among Communist parties. Power can be closely held by those of proven orthodoxy, and regular sessions of "criticism and self-criticism" can be built into the party calendar. Periodic purges, exemplified by Stalin in the Soviet Union or by Mao Tse-Tung's "cultural revolution," will keep party members on their toes. To understate the point, these alternatives are dangerous to democracy. As participation is sharply restricted, leadership grows ever less accessible. A major leader of the Russian Revolution, Leon Trotsky, foresaw this precise development as he wrestled with Lenin and Stalin for control of the Communist party: "The organization of the Party takes the place of the Party itself; the Central Committee takes the place of the organization; and finally the dictator takes the place of the Central Committee."[38]

As American experience has shown, ideological causes need not necessarily decay into dictatorships. From the Populists and the Progressives, to progressive trade unions, to the contemporary blacks' and women's movements, groups can maintain their commitments to democratic participation. The problem, however, is that the participants may well lose their ideological commitments and substitute more limited goals. The Populists' collective goal of social transformation was replaced by the narrow, self-interested objective of the free coinage of silver; Progressive Theodore Roosevelt's insistent call for national renewal became a timid plea for Republican party unity.

The ideological party ultimately may face choices between ideology and democracy. The party can resolve this dilemma by giving up ideology to maintain membership, by maintaining purity while membership decays, or by forcefully insisting that its ideology represents the true interests of a populace infected by "false consciousness." The dilemma still remains, whether resolved by the autocracy practiced by Lenin or the "embourgeoisment" scorned by Michels.

The ideological community faces a second and related problem. Ideological commitment is necessarily based on a faith in the truth of the ideology. The true believer, possessing truth, equates dissent with error and finds it temperamentally difficult to accept opposition. The ideal of a liberal democratic community, however, is that discussion should be unrestrained, that no opinion should be repressed. John Stuart Mill presented the classic argument:

> The peculiar evil of silencing the expression of an opinion is, that it is robbing the human race; posterity as well as the existing generation; those who dissent from the opinion, still more than those who hold it. If the opinion is right, they are deprived of the opportunity of exchanging error for truth; if wrong, they lose, what is almost as great a benefit, the clearer perception and livelier impression of truth, produced by its collision with error.[39]

Democracies do not always sustain Mill's tolerant spirit. Elections are important instruments of majority will but in themselves do not provide assured attention to the concerns of isolated minorities. Indeed mass elections raise the possibility of majority tyranny, as posed by Tocqueville: "When an individual or a party is wronged in the United States, to whom can he apply for redress? If to public opinion, public opinion constitutes the majority; if to the legislature, it represents the majority, and implicitly obeys it; if to the executive power, it is appointed by the majority, and serves as a passive tool in its hands."[40] Even in relatively open societies such as the United States or Great Britain, most people are not willing to fully tolerate some groups, regardless of their commitment to abstract principles of free speech.[41]

Accepting dissenting minorities is still more difficult within ideological communities. The expressive character of these communities induces hostility toward the outsider, not acceptance, for emotional fervor is more easily sustained by attacks on a defined enemy than by devotion to a bill of rights. That hostility was obvious in Lenin's tirades against his political opponents, and it can also be seen, usually less virulently, even in American third parties. Some Populist support was accompanied by racist hostility toward blacks, and nativism affected some Progressives.

The character of the ideological community is more likely to be orthodox than tolerant, but a truly democratic society rejects orthodoxy. In an extreme form, the model of the political party as an ideological community becomes a church, expelling dissenters as heretics. As it moderates its orthodoxy, the ideological party again faces the possibility of a loss of purpose other than electoral victory.

"What shall it profit a man," the sage asked, "if he shall gain the whole world and lose his own soul?" Contemporary parties require an ideological purpose if they are to gain support; they must save their souls if they would win the world of power. At the same time, the search for salvation by an ideological community can distort the parties as instruments of electoral politics. There is no moral profit for parties that save their souls but corrupt the world of democracy.

FIVE

PASSIONATE INTERESTS:
THE URBAN PARTY MACHINE

Sitting at a shoeshine stand in Manhattan in the early twentieth century, a self-educated political philosopher offered a fervent defense of American political parties: "First, this great and glorious country was built up by political parties; second, parties can't hold together if their workers don't get offices when they win; third, if the parties go to pieces, the government they built up must go to pieces; fourth, then there'll be hell to pay."[1] George Washington Plunkitt, the shoe-stand philosopher, was a district leader of Tammany Hall, probably the most notorious of the great urban machines. His discourses, recorded by a bemused reporter, provide a description of this variety of American political parties, partly serious and partly tongue-in-cheek, partly engaging and partly outrageous, partly accurate and partly deceiving.

CHARACTER AND FUNCTIONS OF
THE URBAN MACHINE

Although Plunkitt praised the machine, others condemned it, particularly for the corruption inevitably associated with it. Indeed, research literature on the subject is commonly found in library catalogs under the heading, "Politics—Corruption." Moral condemnation frequently led to political reform movements, which passed through a discouraging life cycle of indignant victory, civic reform, and early defeat by the resuscitated supporters of the spoils system.

This regular revival of the machine suggests that its strength cannot be attributed simply to blatant corruption or to electoral fraud. After all, when out of power, the machine had access neither to the city treasury nor to the unstuffed ballot boxes. Nevertheless, machine rule has frequently dominated political life in American cities, particularly in the late nineteenth and early twentieth centuries. The longevity and the widespread success of party machines require explanation, not simple disdain.

To understand the machines, we must first acknowledge that their development was not an accident but an adaptation to the conditions of American cities. When machines were in their prime, cities were burgeoning in population, providing great opportunities for economic enterprise, and attracting millions of immigrants and migrants from the hinterland; but adequate governmental means to cope with the consequent enormous political and economic strains were lacking.[2]

The machine's dominance was not inevitable—central governmental planning was one possible alternative. Yet if not inevitable, in a period in which the dominant liberal ideology restricted governmental activism, the machine was an available, convenient, and workable system. Even a severe critic recognized this virtue of the machine and its leaders:

> The depredations committed by the boss are made up for, to a certain extent, by a better, more responsible administration. . . . State legislatures, which vote laws, at the bidding of the boss, to swell the resources of patronage, also vote good laws—laws of public utility. . . . Thus, the boss acts as a disciplining force; he exerts it on the whole political community for good as well as for evil.[3]

In its own terms, the machine was interested only in power, jobs, and profit. To accomplish these manifest goals, however, using the terms of social science, the machine performed vital "latent functions," unintentionally meeting essential societal needs.[4] Cutting through the red tape created by overlapping governmental jurisdictions and multiple checks and balances, the machine fostered the building of urban infrastructure, manufacturing, and commerce. Those doing business with the city—utilities, construction companies, suppliers—considered payments to the machines as part of their costs, which were recovered in profitable contracts. For a special category of business, the machine provided a different kind of help; in an age of official puritanism, it protected services that were illegal but still desired, such as liquor, gambling, and prostitution.

The machine also accomplished social as well as economic functions. It achieved the political socialization of new arrivals, making them citizens and voters. It created electoral coalitions among diverse and contentious groups. It softened the harshness of capitalist development by providing a modicum of social welfare for the poor. It provided an alternative mechanism of social mobility for those skilled in the arts of politics, particularly for low-status ethnic groups. In promoting these ends, the spoilsmen forged a rough union of mass democracy and urban growth, doing so inadvertently and often without good intentions. The financial costs were great and ultimately would be paid by the poor, in the coin of limited and inefficient governmental services, high costs, and regressive taxation.

Nevertheless, the work of government did get done: Subways were built to carry the urban work force between new jobs and modest tenements, even as construction costs were inflated by corruption and high profits; children were provided at least minimal literacy, and neighborhood crime was kept in check, even if schoolteachers and policemen were appointed on the basis of personal friendships instead of merit.

THE MACHINE AS A PARTY ORGANIZATION

The machine constitutes a distinctive form of political party but shares some characteristics with other models. Concentrating on gaining benefits for its activists, it has an elite focus; in this respect, it resembles a party bureaucracy. The machine's benefits are essentially discrete individual advantages for the party's workers, most notably the patronage of public office, making the party goals coalitional rather than collective. Based on this criterion, the machine is like a team of office seekers.

Yet machines are different from bureaucracies or office-seeking teams, the critical distinction being in their mode of activity. They are expressive and emotion-laden organizations, not coldly rational power seekers. Machines arouse loyalties and antipathies, a distinctive characteristic, even as they pursue their coalitional goals and develop their elite organizational structures.

The common view of machines regards them as hierarchical organizations, bent on private gain, emphasizing instrumental activities. They are typically portrayed simply as earlier and more colorful versions of contemporary campaign consultants. This view is only partially correct. Although the machine did stress coalitional goals, its internal organization was less cohesive than is generally assumed, and its operational mode is more appropriately seen as expressive rather than as instrumental.

The word "machine" itself suggests a highly disciplined and centralized organization. The descriptive literature identifies these organizations with their imperial "bosses," the legendary names of Tweed, Pendergast, Ruef, Hague, Curley, and Daley.[5] In Philadelphia, identified by Lincoln Steffens as "a very perfect machine," the hierarchy stretched across all formal governmental barriers:

> Matthew S. Quay . . . is the proprietor of Pennsylvania and the real ruler of Philadelphia, just as William Penn, the Great Proprietor, was. . . . The organization that rules Philadelphia is . . . not a mere municipal machine, but a city, State, and national organization. The people of Philadelphia are Republicans in a Republican city in a Republican state in a Republican nation, and they are bound ring on ring on ring. . . . All these bear down upon Philadelphia to keep it in control of Quay's boss and his little ring. This is the ideal of party organization, and, possibly, is the end toward which our democratic republic is tending.[6]

On closer examination, however, these parties seem less hierarchical than suggested by the images of machines and bosses. Their histories are replete with internal conflicts, intrigue, and palace coups. The machine was intensely personal and local, with loyalties tied to individuals, not to the common organization. Rather than a modern bureaucracy, it more closely resembled opportunistic feudalism. Each ward chieftain had his band of followers. The leader of the party held power not by command but by dint of his ability to maintain alliances among these barons. As the fortunes of political war changed, these bands would shift their allegiances as faithlessly as the dukes in Shakespeare's histories. Although some bosses did maintain their power for considerable periods, all of them knew the truth of the playwright's warning, "Uneasy lies the head that wears the crown." Their unease was even greater when they depended on material rewards for their power. In such machines, once these prizes were lost, the boss also lost the source of his authority.

Explanations of the machines' success typically emphasize these material rewards. Even Plunkitt finds such incentives essential to these parties, including patronage jobs and the "honest graft" that politicians gained from inside information. The same emphasis is evident in more academic writings, for example, in the fundamental work of Banfield and Wilson, who unqualifiedly define a machine as "a party organization that depends crucially upon inducements that are both *specific* and *material*. . . . A political machine is a business organization in a particular field of business—getting votes and winning elections."[7]

Illustrations of this emphasis on material incentives, on the instrumental party mode, abound in the rich vocabulary of American politics. We can read about the machine's "boodle," the exploits of the "gas house gang," the reformers' denunciation of party "tyranny." Machine leaders are universally described as inevitably materialistic and despotic. "As with every autocrat, absolute power makes him lose his head sooner or later; he becomes willful, arrogant, and tyrannical; he exceeds all bounds in the effrontery with which he and his men use the public resources for their own benefit."[8] But this emphasis is not fully appropriate. Machines certainly have employed material appeals, but this alone cannot explain their strength and longevity. Empirical research leads to a reconsideration of their mode of operation.

Plunkitt was convinced that "when parties can't get offices they'll bust. They ain't far from the bustin' point now, with all this civil service business keepin' most of the good things from them." His reformist adversaries agreed, although they did not share his further concern, that civil service reform led to the death of patriotism:

How are you goin' to keep up patriotism if this thing goes on? You can't do it. Let me tell you that patriotism has been dying out fast for the last twenty years. Before then when a party won, its workers got everything in sight. . . . The boys and men don't get excited any more when they see a United States flag or hear "The Star-Spangled Banner." And why should they? What is there in it for them?[9]

In assessing the importance of material incentives, however, it is significant that machines were able to resist the alleged damage of civil service reform. Notable leaders of Tammany itself, such as Richard Crocker and Charles Murphy, came to power after, not before, civil service reform, as did the great Chicago organizations of Nash, Kelly, and Daley and smaller machines elsewhere.

The survival of machines, despite civil service reform, can be partially explained by the parties' ability to manipulate and to limit the scope of the reform legislation. In Chicago, for example, "temporary" jobs were exempted from merit systems, and a large proportion of municipal jobs were then classified as temporary, even when held by the same individuals for decades. The ability of the machines to use these stratagems, however, suggests that they had deeper sources of strength than the jobs on the public payroll.[10]

Consider then the simple numbers involved. Even in their heyday, machines did not provide public jobs for all their members. Gosnell and his students did the most thorough investigations, examining Chicago, reputedly the strongest of these party organizations. Even in this most "advanced" specimen of the species, patronage positions were not available for about one-half of the ward leaders, the elite officers of the party, or for more than one-third of the precinct leaders, its street-level troops.[11]

Fewer direct material rewards could be expected in organizations weaker than the Chicago leviathan, yet machines still dominated urban politics. In all cities, rather than having unlimited rewards to distribute, "party bosses had to husband *scarce* resources. The demands of ethnic groups and the working class for jobs and services nearly always exceeded the machine's available supply."[12]

Even though limited in supply, patronage conceivably could strengthen machines if the scarce resource were employed to advance their goals through internal party discipline. In legend, we hear of the allocation of appointments and promotions through a political merit system, as workers competed to carry their precincts, were repaid with low-level jobs, and then advanced on the public-payroll ladder as they achieved more victories for the party. The party then would indeed be a business, using corporate-management standards of job efficiency—measured by electoral, not bureaucratic performance—and matching rewards—the spoils of patronage—to this performance.

In fact, complex social systems, including corporate businesses, do not fit the model of a pure goal-oriented organization.[13] Maintaining social relationships among the members of the organization often becomes more important than its manifest external goals. Personal considerations can displace the impersonal standards of achievement. Traditional practices are maintained long after they have become irrelevant to the original task, and the organization itself may be perpetuated even after it has accomplished its intended mission. These realities are evident to anyone who has seen co-workers "covering" for a well-liked but ineffective colleague or wondered why the military still maintained horse cavalry after tanks were invented. The same "inefficiencies" have been found in empirical studies of party machines' use of material rewards.

Even in the original allocation of jobs, the standards used do not fit a model of efficient politics. With the causes of political success themselves unclear, the reasons for the division of spoils among the winners cannot be closely compared to the relative achievements of the would-be winners. Instead, personal and ethnic criteria, unrelated to electoral results, are applied.[14] Another material reward, the provision of public services among constituents, also has been found to be unconnected to political effort. Bringing in the votes, even in the vaunted Chicago machine, apparently has little relationship to bringing home the bacon of fire protection, parks, and similar amenities.[15]

Once hired, patronage appointees are often politically inactive; indeed, they may drop any political activity in order to protect themselves from the retribution of future winners. Jobs do not stimulate work for the party, then, but actually become a disincentive.[16] Furthermore, advancement and retention do not necessarily depend on political performance back in the precincts. And even in the most mundane patronage appointments, some standards related to the appointive position must be taken into account. Illustratively, a former "reform" leader of Tammany Hall recounts his successful insistence that persons appointed as "hole inspectors," supervising utility work in the city streets, at least be able to see.[17]

Morale among the patronage workers also must be considered. They are likely to view themselves as entitled to their positions because of their original effort for the party. Disciplining these people when their political activity lessens may cause discontent and disruption among the employees, with the result that the patronage system becomes slack.[18]

Rather than being dependent on material rewards, the political machine should be understood as relying substantially, although not exclusively, on affective appeals. This reliance is evident even beneath Plunkitt's cynical veneer, when he applauds the "magnificent men" of the "grand Tammany organization" or praises the "heroism" of party workers at a Fourth of July ceremony: "five thousand men sittin' in the hottest place on earth for four long hours, with parched lips and gnawin' stomachs, and knowin' all the time that the delights of the oasis in the desert were only two flights downstairs."[19]

MACHINES AND VOTERS

Materialism cannot explain the internal operation of the machine; still less can it explain its broad electoral popularity, which allowed it to survive periodic defeats, fissures, and reforms. Even if patronage had been sufficient to satisfy the competing claims of all the precinct activists, certainly no public payroll could have sustained the poor and immigrant populations that repeatedly returned machines to office, even without benefit of ballot fraud.

To be sure, there were some material rewards available to loyal voters — sometimes a job with the gas company if not with the police, or a lowered tax assessment, or the proverbial turkey at Thanksgiving and basket of coal at Christmas. In later periods, machines even turned "reform" to their advantage, finding new jobs for their activists in the regulatory state established with the civil service and new benefits for their constituents in the welfare state created by the New Deal.[20]

Yet even in these extended forms, the machine's material rewards for most of its constituents were usually quite small. It denigrates the poor to believe that they could be bought so cheaply. The true appeal of the machine was not the paltry handouts it provided but the hand it extended. Its strength was best stated by Martin Lomasny of Boston, speaking to Lincoln Steffens: "I think . . . that there's got to be in every ward somebody that any bloke can come to — no matter what he's done — and get help. Help you understand; none of your law and your justice, but help."[21]

The work of the machine was that of good neighbors, concerned with the lives and deaths of their friends. Plunkitt again is illustrative, responding to the plight of a family burned out of its home:

> I don't refer them to the Charity Organization Society, which would investigate their case in a month or two and decide they were worthy of help about the time they are dead from starvation. I just get quarters for them, buy clothes for them if their clothes were burned up, and fix them up till they get things runnin' again.

That work was not morally pure, for there was always an explicit or implied contract in which help was extended in exchange for votes. "It's philanthropy," Plunkitt admits, "but it's politics too — mighty good politics. Who can tell how many votes one of these fires bring me? The poor are the most grateful people in the world, and let me tell you, they have more friends in their neighborhoods than the rich have in theirs."[22] Yet even this contractual relationship carried a certain dignity, for in the contract, the machine politician did not give the voter charity. He made an exchange between two persons, each with resources, the politician providing the favor, the voter providing the ballot.

A particular affective appeal of the machine was ethnicity. It is almost impossible to describe this kind of party organization without adding an adjective such as "Irish" or "Italian" or, recently, "black." But ethnicity is an appeal to the emotions, not to rational calculation; the rewards it provides are not those of material goods but those of social solidarity.

These were the rewards, reaching across ethnic barriers, that Henry Jones Ford saw in the "surprising amount of intimacy and association between people of different nationalities." He painted a somewhat patronizing, perhaps racist, scene of the assimilationist effects of political patronage:

> In the district headquarters of a party organization, one may perchance see an Irish ward captain patting on the back some Italian ward worker who can barely speak intelligible English, but whose pride and zeal in the success of his efforts to bring his compatriots "in line with the party" are blazoned upon his face. American politics seems able to digest and assimilate any race of the Aryan stock, but it fails with the negro race. [23]

In its electoral efforts, the machine consciously used ethnic appeals. Sometimes these appeals promoted social integration, as in the creation of "balanced tickets," including candidates of different ethnic groups. At other times, the machine would play on and exacerbate group differences. Grievances from the Old World, such as those of the English and the Irish, were fought again in the mobilization of Irish immigrants against New England yankees. New World conflicts were added: Irish against Italians (each group, in urban legend, believing the other had the "o" at the wrong end of their names), and later, whites against blacks.

The importance of these appeals has also been shown by empirical examination of the voting support—ethnic, not economic—of the urban machines. There is very little correlation between class position and support of machine candidates in local elections during the period of machine dominance, but there is a high relationship between ethnicity and the machine vote. [24]

Ethnicity defined the boundaries of the urban electorate. Contrary to the prevailing ideology of a homogenized America, the machine went "beyond the melting pot," recognizing the emerging reality of a more diverse nation.[25] Its activists literally spoke the languages of the immigrant populations and participated in the critical events of their life cycles—births, weddings, and funerals—becoming identified not only with individual voters but with their communities. "By their substantive and symbolic activities," even to the present, machine politicians "persuade the voters that they are concerned about the local community and that they are acting to advance its interests."[26]

In attacking the machine, reformers could make a good and rational case regarding its corruption and even its social inequities, but they rarely could overcome these emotional ties. As a result, most reform administrations would be turned out of office after a single term. The notable exceptions—such as Fiorello LaGuardia in New York and Brand Whitlock in Toledo—were reformers who themselves adopted similar ethnic appeals.[27]

Ironically, these same strong affective appeals of ethnicity undermined the machines. As immigrant groups succeeded each other in America's cities, most machines could not adapt to their changing constituencies. The Irish machines that had once fostered quick naturalization and political mobilization of immigrants came to depend on a limited electorate of their kindred and to resist the assimilation of newer immigrants from the more distant parts of Europe or from the American South. While keeping a firm grip on the major proportion of offices and patronage for themselves, Irish machine leaders attempted to hold off the new groups by providing smaller spoils and symbolic rewards. "In the short run, the Irish monopoly of power preserved the machine. In the long run, the failure to share power with later-arriving ethnic groups eroded the organization's electoral base."[28]

A rational organization, of course, would circulate its leadership to appeal to the new ethnic groups, but it happened only rarely. Irish politicians were not succeeded by Italian politicians; they were defeated as the Italians in turn have been defeated by the blacks.[29] The solidary claims of ethnicity proved stronger to the machine than the instrumentalist claims of electoral rationality.

THE MACHINE'S VISION

The goals of the machine were different from its mode of appeal. Its objectives were essentially materialist and individualist, combined for political purposes into a coalitional program. Analyses of the machine correctly emphasize these materialistic goals; they err in seeing the goals as also being the source of its deeper, more affective appeal.

Broad social programs were simply outside the understanding of the machine politician. "The political structure is not based upon people in general," William Whyte explained. "The politician has obligations to particular people, and he maintains his organization by discharging a certain number of these obligations." He might provide recreational facilities, for example, but this social amenity would only be a by-product of distinct individualist objectives, such as the graft to be skimmed from the construction of a park or a favor to individual constituents. In a crowded Boston neighborhood, for instance, a protective fence was not placed around a baseball diamond until an identifiable group of voters made the local leader aware of the direct political benefits.[30]

Individual needs were not aggregated to the social level. The machine would provide immediate, even generous, help to the family that suffered a tenement fire or to the widow whose breadwinner was killed in a factory accident. Yet it rarely had the vision to prevent these disasters by sponsoring legislation to require fire-resistant construction or safer factories. Indeed, such legislation would not clearly benefit the machine because there would then be fewer victimized families and widows and therefore fewer grateful voters.

More generally, the maladies of urban life in the period of the machines were class problems, common disabilities of the poor. The machine, however, found it difficult to conceive of society as composed of social classes or to mobilize voters along class lines. One part of the difficulty stemmed from its unspoken capitalist alliances, solidified with payoffs and deals. As Steffens stressed, machines depended on at least the sufferance, and usually the active support, of the businessman:

> He does not neglect, he is busy with politics, oh very busy and very businesslike. I found him buying boodlers in St. Louis, defending grafters in Minneapolis, originating corruption in Pittsburg, deploring reformers in Chicago, and beating good government with corruption funds in New York.[31]

Sharing individualist, acquisitive goals, the machine and the local robber barons were natural allies.

Beyond simple corruption, the machine showed only a limited ability to articulate the common interests of its constituent groups. The most obvious feature of the machine coalition was its foundation in ethnic groups, but this characteristic could be divisive. Beneath this surface competition were the common needs of the urban working class, as Bridges has shown, and the machine potentially constituted a class response to capitalist development.[32] Yet if the purpose of politics was seen as winning the spoils for the Irish over the Italians, any synthesizing vision of expanding jobs for both segments of the working class was impossible.

This limited view made the machines antagonistic toward class-based organizations and also vulnerable in competition with them. Machines directly attacked working-class parties, sometimes violently, and offered few economic, rather than ethnic, appeals in their campaigns. Labor unions were seen as rivals, not as potential allies, and were often targets of machine repression, most notably by Frank Hague in Jersey City. Even as prominent a politician as New York's Al Smith would find himself repudiated by his machine colleagues when he adopted a broader class perspective.

Ultimately, the limited vision of the machine and its consequent vulnerability became evident as it declined with the onset of the New Deal and the development of the welfare state. Decline came, in one sense, from simple market competition. The demand for welfare became overwhelming with the collapse of the economy and the social deprivations of the Great Depression. As a local, "retail" supplier of relief, the machine could not compete with the federal government's "wholesale" supply of housing, jobs, and income subsidies. In some cities, such as New York, the federal government deliberately used its control of the "welfare market" to weaken the machine.

This competition, however, is not a complete explanation of the machine's decline. In some areas, the machine was able to form an alliance with the new federal agencies, becoming, as it were, the local distributor of the national government's wholesale resources. In Chicago, this literally became the precinct captains' role, when they personally delivered welfare checks.[33] Thus the Chicago machine attempted to put new money into old wallets, to transform a collective benefit into particularized, individual benefits. Adjusting to the new governmental competition, however, required more than convenient alliances. It demanded that the machine abandon its core strengths and find appeals broader than those of friendship, neighborhood, and ethnic group. In effect, its survival required that it commit suicide.

The long-term weakening of the machine was a subtle process, resulting from the substitution of class for ethnic relationships and of objective standards for personal ones.[34] Federal aid was given to poor people as a category and to those who met stated criteria. Old-age pensions, for example, were established through the social security system for all the elderly, not just the Irish widows befriended by the precinct captain. If direct governmental aid no longer carried with it the captain's warmth of human concern, it also no longer carried with it the burden of political obligation.

To be sure, political intervention could still be helpful, particularly in prodding the bureaucracy. In the role of advocate or ombudsman, however, the machine politician had less power of his own. A cycle of impotence ensued: The bureaucracy became more autonomous and more efficient; the machine politician lost influence within government; voters had less reason to seek his help; and the power of bureaucracy grew further. The machine's passing was marked, but with little notice of the irony, when modern urban administrations established "little city halls" to provide residents with neighborhood help in dealing with the government. The bureaucracy not only had defeated the machine; it had replaced it with its own imitation.

In its stress on coalitional goals, the machine carried the seeds of its own destruction. As it replaced the earlier elites, it also lost their communitarian or "mutualist" view of politics and instead saw voters as individuals or as members of small and distinct groups, competing in a "militant" politics.[35] It could not envision them as members of a social collective, such as the poor or the working class. When other agencies could meet these individualist goals better, the machine had no broader or more inspiring ideals. Similarly, it saw businessmen only as profiteers. When business abandoned declining urban enterprises, it could not join with them to enrich the city rather than the corporation.

The problems of the machine were ultimately problems of internal contradictions in its practice and in its thought: an elite focus versus a mass base; individualistic, coalitional goals versus social, collective needs; ethnic particularism versus class needs. The same problems still limit the possibility of a revival of the urban machine.

In contemporary American politics, machines are treated like animals in a museum: rare, preserved for scholarly examination, but possibly capable of resurrection. If there is to be a revival of urban machines, it will surely be based on black and other minorities, the growing population groups in the nation's cities. Blacks have come to power in virtually every major city, even where they were not a majority of the population, such as in Los Angeles and New York.

Machine parties might be expected in these cities, for the needs that the machines once met are again evident among the nonwhite population. Opportunities for economic profit are available, business still wants favorable treatment, the poor and disadvantaged require social welfare, patronage jobs can provide a living, personal consideration is always in short supply. The newer urbanites have taken the places of the old, with similar needs and with even more reason to respond to the affective appeals of ethnicity.

Other requisites for the machine's success, however, are less evident. Fewer resouces are available to any putative machine. Civil service, the growth of employees' unions, judicial restraints, and bureaucratic insulation make fewer jobs available. Economic wealth has shifted away from the cities so that businesses must be persuaded to invest in cities rather than strong-armed into political contributions. As government has become larger and more technical, parties have lost many of their functions to professional experts, such as social workers, and have been restricted by bureaucratic procedures, such as closed bidding on construction contracts.

New machines, even if feasible, still face the old internal contradictions. Providing patronage jobs for blacks or Hispanics may correct a historic injustice, but it does not constitute a program of social improvement. Ethnic mobilization of "people of color" does not solve the problems of the poor who are white any more than mobilization of the Irish solved the problems of the poor who were Italian, Jewish, and Negro. Machine protection of drug dealers in minority ghettos helps their residents as little as earlier protection of bootleggers helped white tenement dwellers.

Broad programs of urban redevelopment still require collective action and extensive popular support, not a simple redistribution of limited benefits to active but myopic precinct captains. Effective black machines will not only have to be as efficient as their white predecessors; they will also need to be smarter.

MACHINES AND THE DEMOCRATIC FUTURE

The machine form of party organization paralleled a particular kind of democracy, evidencing coalitional goals, an autonomous leadership, and extensive participation. The machine made some contributions to democracy, but it was an incomplete democracy. Coalitional goals limited the possibility of collective action and the emergence of programs to deal with common problems of the poor or the working class, or, today, of the racially disadvantaged. Contemporary cities cannot serve their populations by individual relief but require concerted programs toward some vision of the common good.

The machine's failure ultimately resulted from the absence of such philosophic vision. It saw voters essentially as acquisitive individuals; it could not consider them in the more abstract role of citizen. The patriotism Plunkitt praised was not truly a commitment to the nation and to its common good but only to the private advantages that might be gained. Thus Plunkitt could not even understand, much less answer, John Kennedy's famous challenge, "Ask not what your country can do for you, ask what you can do for your country."

Participation under the machine was widespread, but for most voters, it was still limited to a periodic endorsement of its ethnic leaders. Although the machine offered opportunities for entry and advancement to lower-status groups, it did so only for a few people. Even for these party workers, their extensive activity was not only morally dubious, it was politically corrosive. In these respects, contemporary urban politics shows little improvement.

The greatest defect of the machine was not its corruption; it was most deficient in its training in citizenship. The machine did teach the rudimentary means of democratic politics, bringing its constituents to the polls, "assisting" them in casting a ballot, helping them to organize. It also aroused the emotional loyalties that democratic participation requires. But it was inherently unable to teach the broader meaning of citizenship, the involvement of self in a larger social enterprise.

In the cities of the machine, public life became no more than a bigger and better-endowed arena for private satisfaction. These urban areas contrasted starkly with an earlier city, classical Athens. There, Pericles boasted, "Each individual is interested not only in his own affairs but in the affairs of the state as well"; there, he could realistically urge his audience "that you should fix your eyes every day on the greatness of Athens as she really is, and should fall in love with her."[36] Without this love beyond the self, the machines inevitably perished. Without it, whatever the leadership, democracy itself cannot long survive.

SIX

INTERESTS AND PASSIONS: PARTY AS RATIONAL TEAM AND PERSONAL FACTION

> By the principle of utility is meant that principle which approves or disapproves of any action whatsoever, according to the tendency which it appears to have to augment or diminish the happiness of the party whose interest is in question. . . . When matters of such importance as pain and pleasure are at stake, . . . who is there who does not calculate? Men calculate, some with less exactness, indeed, some with more: but all men calculate.
> —Jeremy Bentham[1]

> Thus politicians in our model never seek office as a means of carrying out particular policies; their only goal is to reap the rewards of holding office *per se*. They treat policies purely as a means to the attainment of their private ends, which they can reach only by being elected.
> —*Anthony Downs*[2]

All political parties seek power, and all democratic parties seek to win elections. The model of parties as rational teams of office seekers is notable for its particular stress on the winning of elections; it seeks to explain party behavior with this single premise. Among the models examined in this book, it posits a particularly close relationship between the party and the mass electorate. Both groups are assumed to have a similar motivation, the advancement of their particular interests.

The concept of party as a rational team is a principal model of American politics. It provides insight into party functioning while stimulating research. At the same time, as a deductive model, it cannot be expected to explain all American political realities. Its purpose is to establish a small number of abstract assumptions and hypotheses that can then be used to better explain the more complicated empirical world. Furthermore, a deductive model should not be viewed as a moral statement. The assumption of self-interest of the office-seeking model is not a normative endorsement of self-interested behavior; it is meant to be only an explanation of how politics operates. The model, however, does raise difficult questions about the nature and purpose of democracy.

The political party of the rational team model has certain distinctive characteristics. Its focus is the mass electorate, whose preferences determine the actions of an accessible elite; this mass focus distinguishes the team model from that of a bureaucratic organization. Considerations of the internal character of the party are largely disregarded. In his theory, Downs sets aside any consideration of the internal interactions of party activists by positing that they tacitly "agree on all their goals."

The party team, furthermore, has no independent ideology, in contrast to a governing caucus or an ideological community, since its purpose is simply the winning of office. In its emphasis on coalitional goals, it resembles the urban machine; it is distinct, however, in that the machine's expressive mode is different from this model's instrumental mode.

THE CONCEPT OF A PARTY TEAM

The basic premises of this model are found in the political theory of utilitarianism, as developed by such nineteenth-century British writers as Jeremy Bentham. Essentially, the utilitarian theory sees humans as seeking individual satisfactions: "Nature has placed mankind under the governance of two sovereign masters, *pain* and *pleasure*. It is for them alone to point out what we ought to do, as well as to determine what we shall do."[3] Bentham argues that rational individuals, in considering any action, calculate four aspects of the pleasures and pains of each alternative: intensity, duration, certainty, and remoteness. When the calculations are completed, a rational individual will choose that course of action which provides him with the highest net gain in intense, long-lasting, certain, and immediate pleasure. Government, in determining public policy, Bentham urges, should employ similar calculations while adding one other consideration, the number of persons who would be pleased or pained by any action. It would then choose those policies that produce "the greatest happiness of the greatest number."[4]

Anthony Downs, in originating the model of political parties as rational teams of office seekers, applies utilitarian theory to political parties. To develop his model, Downs begins by assuming a perfectly informed voter. Under these admittedly unrealistic conditions,

> Each citizen casts his vote for the party he believes will provide him with more benefits than any other. . . . Since one of the competing parties is already in power, its performance in [the current time] period

gives him the best possible idea of what it will do in the future. . . .
As a result, the most important part of a voter's decision is the size of
his *current party differential*, i.e., the difference between the [ben-
efits] he actually received in [the current] period and the one he would
have received if the opposition had been in power.[5]

These voter calculations, as we shall discuss more fully in chapter 7, are
affected by such factors as events, candidates, party loyalty, and particular
policy issues. Our present interest is in the political parties, which have
their own goal, winning office. To achieve this goal, and assuming they
have full knowledge of the political situation, parties engage in another
calculation of voters' pleasures and pains:

Because the government in our model wishes to maximize political
support, it carries out those acts of spending which gain the most votes
by means of those acts of financing which lose the fewest votes. . . .
Under these radically oversimplified conditions, the government subjects each decision to a hypothetical poll and always chooses the alternative which the majority of voters prefer.[6]

A principal characteristic of this model of party is its responsiveness to
the electorate. The party team is defined as a unified group who "act solely
in order to attain the income, prestige, and power which come from being
in office."[7] In the real world, as Downs recognizes, there are other motives.

In their search for power, parties also take on certain principles, but they
acquire principles almost accidentally, as necessary means to the end of
electoral victory. In these parties, "leaders are anxiously scanning the hori-
zon hoping for a breeze to fill their sails." Voters gain influence in this
system because the winning party, "organized to get office and to manage
government, absorbs popular principles and fights valiantly for their
realization."[8]

The parties operate in a political market, trying to win "customers," just
as corporations do in selling their goods. In the simplified situation of complete information, the parties will just follow majority will on all issues,
and their policies will be quite similar; however, this situation is neither true
nor interesting. In the real world, both voters and parties have uncertain
and incomplete information: Voters cannot gain enough information to cast

a fully rational vote, and parties cannot always know the voters' preferences.

Recognizing the voters' uncertainties, the parties employ various strategies. They will stress party loyalty empty of policy content, hoping to make gains on the basis of "brand name loyalty." They will appeal to "passionate minorities," those who hold a minority view on a particular issue of public policy but cast their vote only on this single issue. They will give special attention to vocal interest groups that claim to speak for significant numbers of voters. Parties will also be responsive to financial contributors, who can provide the resources to reach and convince uncertain voters. Another strategy is to cloud the party's position in a vague ideology to attract voters of all varieties. "Ambiguity thus increases the number of voters to whom a party may appeal. This fact encourages parties in a two-party system to be as equivocal as possible about their stands on each controversial issue."[9]

These strategies, born of the inevitability of uncertainty, have two paradoxical results. First, they stimulate differences in the policy positions of the parties, a prerequisite of democratic choice among alternatives. Because the parties cannot be sure of the voters' true preferences, they will take risks, accepting the claims of opinion minorities and of interest groups. They may win power in this way, but it is logically possible that this process could result in a government that represents the minority opinion on each particular issue. How then can this government claim the democratic legitimacy of majority rule?

The second paradox results from inherent tension between the interests of the parties and those of the voters. The parties' interest often is in avoiding commitment on policy issues in order to win votes. They can do so by creating ambiguity on issues, using vague ideologies, or relying on appeals of personality. The voters' interest is in clear policy alternatives so that they can increase their benefits from government. Thus the political parties, the apparent instruments of democratic opinion, can actually frustrate the will of the democratic electorate.

Schlesinger has extended the Downsian model. Although sharing Downs's emphasis on the party as an office-seeking organization, he elaborates on the organizational characteristics of this form of political party. Schlesinger compares parties to other organizations, particularly to corporations and government bureaucracies. Parties do share a market orientation with corporations (although their market is political rather than economic), but they are distinctive in two other dimensions. Parties deal with public rather than with private goods. In this respect, they are different from corporations but akin to bureaucracies. Parties also provide only indirect compensation for most of their members (such as the joy of victory or preferred public policies) rather than direct payments (such as salaries). In this respect they are different from both corporations and bureaucracies.[10]

As comprehensive explanations, the models of party as rational team developed by Downs and Schlesinger provide great insight into the characteristics of American parties. They enable us to understand changes in the parties that are occurring as the result of shifts in partisan competition, political incentives, and the character of party identification. Yet these models present problems, both in their internal coherence and in their implications for democratic theory.

THE RATIONAL PARTY IN THE AMERICAN ENVIRONMENT

A traditional description of American political parties depicts them as "loose, supple, interest-directed, principle-shunning, coalition-forming," characterized by "the decentralization of authority in the organization of these parties in the country at large" and evidencing an "absence of effective discipline in the organization of these parties within the government."[11] Though accepting the description, critics have also denounced American parties for precisely these characteristics.

The model of the rational party team informs us that these characteristics do not result from perverse choices of willful party leaders. Rather, given the particular institutional frameworks of American politics, these traits are the logical results of the parties' search for power, that is, of their basic nature. The absence of commitment to ideological principle follows from the first axiom of the model that defines the party as a seeker after office. Similarly, the interest coalitions embraced within the party can be understood as the result of party efforts to assemble a winning majority in conditions of uncertainty.

Decentralization, Schattschneider writes, "constitutes *the most important single fact concerning the American parties*. He who knows this fact, and knows nothing else, knows more about American parties than he who knows everything except this fact."[12] The traditionally decentralized nature of American parties results from the characteristics of their political "market." For the sake of simplicity, Downs posits a single national political official who makes all policy decisions. In the American system, the reality is that many offices will be the objects of political ambition.

Parties in the United States are necessarily incohesive. They seek to elect not only a president but thousands of officials: municipal council members, state legislators and governors, members of Congress—not to mention county and school boards, judges, and state administrators. Not only are there many offices but, crucially, they are politically independent of one another in important respects. They are elected on different calendars, at different times, from different constituencies. Each of these positions can constitute an "office nucleus" for party competition.[13]

Furthermore, the constitutional system designedly creates clashing interests between those who hold power in different offices. Politicians cannot be trusted, we presume; to keep them under control, they should be made to fight one another. They are elected separately, holding their power for fixed terms, and therefore are free to fight, uninhibited by any immediate threat of losing office. "Checks and balances" is the polite language for this incitement to conflict. The Constitution embodies "this policy of supplying, by opposite and rival interests, the defect of better motives . . . where the constant aim is to divide and arrange the several offices in such a manner as that each may be a check on the other—that the private interest of every individual may be a sentinel over the public rights."[14]

In these conditions, if parties are to be considered as teams, they are of a distinct variety. They are different from a model football squad, with each player fulfilling a specific assignment, following the orders of the quarterback or the coach, with points awarded only for collective effort. They sometimes resemble baseball teams, where individuals can achieve recognition and considerable rewards, but championship play requires cooperative effort. Increasingly, American parties are more like swimming clubs, where members typically compete as individuals and only occasionally in relays, where each competitor swims her own race, and where the team's points are simply the arithmetic sum of these individual accomplishments.

Decentralization is the rational party team's response to American conditions. It allows politicians to pursue their presumed self-interest in winning office while adjusting to the local conditions of the political market.

Strategies can be altered to promote victory for a particular office in a particular area, for example, by recruiting Mormon candidates in Utah or by emphasizing mass-media campaigning in the enormous California constituency.

Personal style will also vary, not randomly, but in ways that meet political needs. Given their perceptions of different constituencies, "Congressman A seeks out person-to-person relationships, but does not encourage issue-oriented meetings, Congressman D seeks out issue-oriented meetings, but does not encourage person-to-person relationships. . . . Representatives C and E both claim that handshaking is the best way to win votes. Yet Congressman C struggles to meet 'the folks' one on one, whereas Congressman E often chooses presentational techniques that avoid face-to-face relationships with others."[15]

Beyond campaign techniques, decentralization allows and encourages diversity in policy positions rather than the united positions assumed by Downs. As Turner put it in the distant 1950s, "Only a Democrat who rejects a part of the Fair Deal can carry Kansas, and only a Republican who moderates the Republican platform can carry Massachusetts."[16]

Each individual politician acts as utilitarian theory posits, seeking electoral victory. Consistent with the theory, that goal dominates any possible concern for achieving an overall party program. In Congress, the basic rule followed by representatives is "vote your district." Consequently, party unity in government must be constructed from the individual ambitions of officeholders. Sometimes, such ambition promotes loyalty to party, locally reinforced by ideological activists voting in party primaries; at other times, local and party loyalties clash. Legislators do in fact usually vote the same way as their fellow partisans, but they do so only after they are convinced that their votes are either unimportant to voters in their own districts or in keeping with local opinion.[17]

Emphasis on individual candidates is another characteristic of American politics fostered by decentralization. Although this feature is slighted in Downs's policy-oriented model, it is not inconsistent. Since basically the model is one of individual behavior, the actions of individual candidates are explicable on these same premises.

Candidates, according to utilitarian theory, will always follow those political rules that increase their chances of winning office. Their strategies will depend on how they can maximize their opportunities within the structures of politics and on their expectations of voter behavior. To win votes, a candidate minimally requires nomination, money, and campaign organization.

In earlier American politics, these prerequisites were supplied largely through the formal party organization. Nominations, even for president, were made at party conclaves through negotiation among the organization's leaders. Money was supplied by donations to and expenditures by the party organization. Campaigning was conducted by party loyalists emphasizing local, interpersonal contacts. Candidates sought their own goals by learning a simple genealogy. "An effective political party needs five things: offices, jobs, money, workers, and votes. Offices beget jobs and money; jobs and money beget workers; workers beget votes; and votes beget offices."[18]

Contemporary opportunities are essentially independent of party structures. Nominations are largely made by direct primaries, allowing candidates unmediated access to the voters. This legal heritage of the Progressive period is probably the most important single factor in the weakening of party control over nominations, but its effect is not inevitable, for parties have sometimes been able to dominate primaries.[19]

The full effect of the primaries comes from parallel changes in voters' attitudes, their lessened loyalty to party leaders, and their increased receptivity to the candidates' characteristics other than their records of party service. New means of communication with voters, particularly television and other mass media, allow candidates to emphasize these different characteristics.

Essential to any candidate's strategy is money, and some trends in American politics have increased this need. Campaigning through the mass media is more expensive than campaigning by personal contact, as "capital-intensive" politics replaces "labor-intensive" politics. Moreover, the financial costs of campaigning are more overt. When politics was conducted through parties, some of the costs were hidden, as patronage appointees were in effect paid from the public treasury for their campaign work or as special interests bribed legislators. Today, campaign services must be paid for in hard and reported currency, and bribes are probably less common.

Money to pay the greater and more direct costs of campaigning also follows a different route, going directly to candidates rather than through parties. The new financial path facilitates the independence of office seekers from their putative party "teammates." The true impact of political action committees (PACs) has been in their reinforcement of this independence. Although PACs also contribute to the political parties, both the law and these committees' interest in gaining influence encourage direct contributions to the candidates. In a reinforcing cycle of partisan incohesion, office begets power independent of the party, power begets money, money begets votes, and votes beget more independent power.

This trend is commonly referred to as "candidate-centered" campaigning, but the label is somewhat misleading. Democratic elections are frequently focused on the traits and qualities of individual candidates, whether they seek the distinctive office of a president or lead a party seeking a parliamentary majority. Even in periods of greater party dominance in the United States, campaigns still centered on the qualities of an "Old Hickory" Jackson or an "Honest Abe" Lincoln. Campaign biographies illustrate this emphasis on individual personalities.[20] The more novel aspect of modern campaigning is that the candidates' organizations are more central to the actual work of politics, such as raising the money and developing the messages sent to voters.

The changing structure of the candidates' opportunities depends on—and affects—corresponding changes in voter behavior. Candidates place less emphasis on their party label and party service because voters are less responsive to partisanship as a cue in making their electoral decisions. In the nineteenth century, party loyalty was very strong, and a candidate's party label was virtually all a voter asked about before casting his ballot. This was the time, to Jensen, of "military" political parties:

> The parties were army-like organizations, tightly knit, disciplined, united. All the voters, save for a few stragglers and mercenaries, belonged to one or the other army, and the challenge of the campaign was the mobilization of the full party strength at the polls on election day. To heighten the morale of the troops, the generals employed brass-band parades, with banners, badges, torches and uniforms. Chanting sloganized battle cries, waving placards and flags, the rank and file marched for hours before smiling, waving politicians, who invariably thought the men would appreciate a two-hour speech.[21]

Contemporary political parties draw less loyalty, even less interest, and that same lack of passion is evident in actual behavior. Voters defect from their traditional party, split tickets, producing inconsistent results in any given election, and change their party vote from one election to another, causing great volatility in the vote.

Other cues have taken the place of partisanship. As early as the end of the nineteenth century, a new "merchandising" style of politics emerged. Moving closer to the behavior expected in the rational team model, "the platforms and slogans of the parties became less of an army-style device to encourage morale and more of an intellectual appeal to the needs and wants of the voters supplemented by direct, tangible benefits like pensions."[22]

Contemporary campaigning carries this trend forward to the end of the twentieth century, with the particularistic appeals to voters now made by individual candidates. Instead of partisanship, candidates will emphasize personal traits. Especially important in contemporary politics is the cue of incumbency. In Congress, members have become virtually tenured, with less turnover than in the hereditary House of Lords in Great Britain or in the erstwhile "totalitarian" Soviet Politburo of the 1980s.

Reelection of incumbents affects party organization, since secure legislators have less reason to cooperate with other members of the party team. Legislators reinforce their positions by providing discrete benefits to voters, such as services for individual constituents or legislation for favored contributors.[23] The crucial advantage held by incumbents, particularly in the House, is in the information that voters have. The electorate usually knows something about current officeholders but not as much about challengers. In a world of limited interest and uncertain knowledge about politics, incumbency provides sufficient information to direct the voting decision.[24]

The impact of incumbency illustrates how the party as an office-seeking team is affected by the direction and strength of partisanship. When partisanship is high, the parties will be only imperfect competitors. Each party is assured of a certain proportion of votes and need compete only for the remainder. Futhermore, if one party is dominant among committed voters, there is no true competition; it is assured of victory, and its opposition faces certain defeat.

The strength of party commitment is another dimension of partisanship, different from its direction of pro-Democratic or pro-Republican. Lesser commitment, along with increased interparty competition, will affect the organization and campaign style of the parties. When commitment to party is high, the party need pay little attention to persuading voters; only the reinforcement and turnout efforts of "military" parties are necessary. When commitment lessens, the proportion of self-declared Independents or weak partisans will grow. Parties then must work harder for votes and will therefore increase their persuasive or "merchandising" efforts.

Other effects are likely within the party organization. One possibility is that the parties divide, as vulnerable office seekers look for protective cover, avoid controversial policy stands, and neglect larger interests of their party or their governmental institution. In fostering their own interests, members of Congress, for example, "tend their own constituency relations and even attack Congress from time to time to reenforce their customized political support at home."[25] As politicians search for shifting majorities among the electorate, they may find it more difficult to hold their party team together.

Some countervailing trends occur, with increased competition bringing party teammates closer. Legislators show more cooperation in campaigning and display greater cohesion in roll-call voting, and leaders have a fuller role in both policy-making and electioneering. As office seekers face stronger opposition, they also need more friends. "Candidates need all the help they can get; they are finding that the best place to get it is from their fellow partisans."[26] Fuller cooperation does not make the party leaders an integrated team, however; they are closer allies but not yet true mates.

THE PARTY AS PERSONAL FACTION

The American political party has become less like a team and more like a collection of personal coalitions. These candidate organizations are generally instrumental in character and can be described simply as small-scale rational teams. In fewer cases, candidate coalitions begin to resemble a different party model, that of the personal faction, where passions displace interests. In that model, candidates are not only at the center of a campaign, they also exemplify the expressive mode. Some contemporary candidates, Jesse Jackson for example, do arouse such passionate backing.

The hallmark of the personal faction is its emotional loyalty to its leader. The leader expresses some policy orientations, but these are not the crucial elements of his (almost always masculine) appeal, which is based more on his personal characteristics, the way in which the leader appears to embody the hopes, and more often the fears and resentments, of the followers. In the true meaning of the word, the leader of a personal faction has "charisma," the "gift of grace," which legitimizes his power and his program.[27] Because of this personal legitimacy, the leader can change a program without endangering his power. The more extreme examples of personal factions are the totalitarian party movements developed by such figures as Hitler, Mussolini, and the successive Perons. In these parties, "leadership" itself becomes the principle, the basis for expressive and submissive participation.

Although these parties present collective programs, they are little more than nationalistic slogans, such as Mussolini's call for an Italian "place in the sun" or Hitler's genocidal war against the Jews. The real program is personal power, built on compensations to diverse groups in a shifting coalition, such as Hitler's rewards of construction contracts to industrialists, employment for the working class, weapons for the military, and psychological solace for defeat in World War I.[28]

Personal factions also exist in democracies, indeed can be found within almost any large democratic political party. Because politics inevitably involves passions as well as interests, organizations will sometimes center on the magnetic candidate or party leader, with lesser concern for instrumental rewards. The loyalists who gather around the Kennedy family within the Democratic party or those who followed Barry Goldwater or Ronald Reagan in the political wilderness expressed their love of a person more than their commitment to a program. Such devotion is appealing but politically deficient, as can be seen in comparing the personal faction to party as a rational team. Loyalty, like love, can be blind and can lead the devout to electoral defeat. Chicago machine Democrats revealed the problem when they fervently chanted Richard Daley's praises, even as his machine decayed from within. Kennedy loyalists have sometimes seemed to prefer a return to the Camelot of the 1960s over Democratic party victory.

The personal faction limits the opportunity for democratic control. Devotion may allow the leader so much discretion that the electorate has no meaningful influence over public policy. Even more inevitably, a party faction lacks continuity. An office-seeking team inherently must assume the responsibility for the actions of its party teammates, and this continuity allows the electorate to employ rational criteria in voting. Personal factions, in contrast, are only personal and make it difficult for the electorate to hold their leaders accountable on any long-term basis.

DEMOCRACY AND THE RATIONAL PARTY TEAM

The rational party model provides considerable insight into the workings of parties in democracy, even amid doubts about its empirical validity.

Inevitably, the model also raises normative issues, as does the related philosophical theory of utilitarianism. These theories are completely individualistic, seeing each voter as an abstract and isolated rational actor. Bentham wrote, "One man is worth just the same as another man" and calculated utility by the dictum, "Everybody to count for one, nobody for more than one."[29] Beyond individuals, there is no general interest. "The community is a fictitious *body*, composed of the individual persons who are considered as constituting as it were its *members*. The interest of the community then is, what?—the sum of the interests of the several members who compose it."[30]

Similarly, the voting calculations hypothesized by Downs are isolated measurements of individual benefits and costs. This simplifying assumption reflects democratic ideology in one respect, because it presumes complete equality among persons. In fact, however, this premise violates the reality that people are not isolated individuals but live within social groups and communities and reflect these social characteristics in their voting as much as in the other aspects of their lives.

The individualistic premise is also morally dubious, for it seems to encourage egotism and a lack of concern for our fellow humans. If life consists only of individual pleasures and pains, we cannot justify a concern for *others'* pleasures and pains. To avoid this problem, we can define altruism as a source of individual pleasure and social misery as a source of individual pain. This philosophical solution, however, is only a definitional device; if individualism includes everything, it precisely means nothing.

John Stuart Mill, in his revision of Bentham, attempted to include altruistic behavior within utilitarian theory. The standard to be applied, Mill declared, "is not the agent's own happiness, but that of all concerned. As between his own happiness and that of others, utilitarianism requires him to be strictly impartial as a disinterested and benevolent spectator."[31]

In his amendment of utilitarianism, however, Mill loses the simplicity—or oversimplicity—of Bentham's observational rules, substituting normative standards of behavior. As Warnock points out, "Although it may well be that Mill's altruistic principle of utility is a good principle to use, there is nothing to suggest that every one uses it nor that it is the only possible principle."[32]

Downs also recognizes the problem of limiting voters' utility to their narrow personal interests and attempts to include social perspectives in his model. In deciding whether to vote at all, he suggests, a rational citizen may cast a vote for no other reason than "a sense of social responsibility," which can be encompassed in the utilitarian calculus as a long-term benefit derived from "the desire to see democracy work."[33] Futhermore, he concedes, "Men are not always selfish, even in politics. They frequently do what appears to be individually irrational because they believe it is socially rational—i.e., it benefits others even though it harms them personally."[34]

There are logical problems in this analysis because it broadens the definition of benefits to include potentially any motivation. Social responsibility can be invoked as inducing citizens to take the trouble to vote, despite their individualistic interest in limiting their costs in time and acquiring information. This explanation ultimately becomes no more than a self-verifying truism: People vote because they find some reason to vote.[35] Once present at the polls, following this logic, citizens can be seen as rational even when they vote against their individual interests. They might ignore their desires to limit their financial costs and support redistribution of their personal income to the poor, or they might even support suicidal wars, voting against their interest in preserving their lives. More generally, if actions defined by the model as irrational can be made rational simply by definition, the entire notion of rationality becomes a tautology.

The problem with utilitarianism is deeper than these questions of definition. The core purpose of government is to deal with social problems, whether defined as narrowly as protecting private rights (as in Locke) or as broadly as achieving the good society (as in Plato). Concentrating on individual pains and pleasures, however defined, does not necessarily achieve these purposes. For example, environmental quality or public health eventually does affect all persons. The control of air pollution or the prevention of infectious disease, however, requires governmental actions even though the individual beneficiaries of these actions cannot be specifically identified.

Democratic government is even more complicated because all citizens are involved, at least in some minimal fashion, in dealing with these problems. In casting votes, they are affecting not only their own lives but those of others and are therefore morally implicated in the fate of others. At its best, democracy makes people more aware of this implication. By stressing distinct and selfish interests, however, utilitarianism undermines these common interests.[36]

A consistent pursuit of utilitarian, individual goals can also harm the rational party itself. The members of the party team win office on the basis of their satisfaction of popular policy demands. Yet if they pursue their individualistic goals, they will be less likely to cooperate, less successful in solving problems, and ultimately less likely to win office.

Divisiveness within an office-seeking party is especially likely in a time of weakened partisanship, such as the contemporary period in American politics. Ultimately, such divided parties will harm not only their own electoral prospects but their nation. Unsure of votes and of office, with voter revolts a constant threat, they will find it difficult to maintain a steady, consistent course of governmental policy. Yet democracies particularly require consistent leadership, writes Tocqueville, for "a democracy can only with great difficulty regulate the details of an important undertaking, persevere in a fixed design, and work out its execution in spite of serious obstacles."[37] Without steady leadership, democratic opinion may justify Walter Lippmann's mournful description as "too late with too little, or too long with too much, too pacifist in peace and too bellicose in war, too neutralist or appeasing in negotiation or too intransigent."[38]

These effects would be exaggerated if a rational party focused only on winning office, but fortunately political parties do not care only about success. That democracies have not fallen apart is to some extent the result of a steadiness and a sensibility in public opinion.[39] It is also the result of the deliberate actions of party politicians, who have not simply sought victory but who, at least on occasion, have been concerned with the feelings and fates of their teammates and with the interests of their nation. These programmatic emphases have increased within American parties, as party leaders "do not merely act in their own self interest" but also "take positions because they believe it is the appropriate decision to make based on their party and group ties."[40]

Without concern for issues as more than strategies, a political party is not only empty; it is also eventually futile and self-defeating. Leadership is required as well as gain, and the combination is not impossible. Weber provides this basic lesson for politicians:

Certainly all historical experience confirms the truth—that man would not have attained the possible unless time and again he had reached out for the impossible. But to do that a man must be a leader, and not only a leader but a hero as well, in a very sober sense of the word. And even those who are neither leaders nor heroes must arm themselves with that steadfastness of heart which can brave even the crumbling of all hopes. . . . Only he who in the face of all this can say "In spite of all!" has the calling for politics.[41]

SEVEN
PARTY CONCEPTS AND VOTING BEHAVIOR

I seen my opportunities and I took them.
— *George Washington Plunkitt*[1]

The role of the people is to produce a government . . . [in] free competition
among would-be leaders for the vote of the electorate.
— *Joseph Schumpeter*[2]

Diversity marks our analysis of eight different concepts of political parties. These parties do share one basic similarity, the desire to win elections, to take their opportunities, to acquire power in the competitive struggle at the ballot box. Since party victory at the polls requires voter support, the political validity of these concepts must be tested against the realities of electoral behavior.

Different parties will expect voters to behave in different ways. The relationships of the party models to four features of voter behavior are considered in this chapter. The first feature is turnout, the mobilization of voters; the other three are explanations of voters' decisions: partisanship, issue preferences, and candidate characteristics.[3] We will first examine the expectations of voter behavior implicit in the voter models, using historical examples of each model in practice, and then compare these expectations to the empirical realities of contemporary American electoral behavior.

PARTIES AND VOTERS

Needing voters, parties work to influence their participation and perceptions. Like an army in a military campaign, a party in a political campaign will be most likely to win if it can choose the terms of combat. It tries to bring its supporters to the polls, tries to present its candidates as credible and attractive, tries to get voters to concentrate on its preferred issues, and tries to get voters to evaluate it favorably—seeing its past record in a good light and believing its promises for the future.

Much of party campaign strategy is directed toward shaping these voter perceptions. Illustratively, in the 1988 presidential contest Michael

Dukakis might well have been elected if he could have focused the voters' attention on the economic issues of unemployment and the budget deficit, issues on which he held a decided advantage over George Bush. The Republican candidate won not because he prevailed in a debate on those issues but because he successfully focused the campaign on other issues, specifically on defense, crime, and individual taxation.[4]

More generally, parties will emphasize those factors that serve their own cause. Having been the majority party in voter identification for the past fifty years, Democrats will stress partisanship in their campaigns. Countering, Republicans will emphasize policy preferences and individual performance. The summary appeals of the candidates in the 1980 television debate between Jimmy Carter and Ronald Reagan exemplify Democratic and Republican arguments:

> Carter: I think this debate . . . typifies . . . the basic historical differences between the Democratic Party and the Republican Party. . . . These commitments that the Democratic Party has historically made to the working families of this nation, have been extremely important. . . . So, it is good for the American people to remember that there is a sharp basic historical difference between Governor Reagan and me on these crucial issues—also, between the two parties that we represent.
>
> Reagan: Next Tuesday is Election Day. . . . I think when you make that decision, it might be well if you would ask yourself, are you better off than you were four years ago? Is it easier for you to go and buy things in the stores than it was four years ago? Is there more or less unemployment in the country than there was four years ago? Is America as respected throughout the world as it was? Do you feel that our security is as safe, that we're as strong as we were four years ago?[5]

In choosing their strategies, however, parties do not have unlimited discretion. Incumbent candidates will be judged primarily by their performance, not their promises, as nonincumbents will be assessed by the reverse standards.[6] Candidates may try to draw favorable images of themselves, but their experience in public office and their past positions are readily available for publicity and possible exploitation by their opposition.

Parties also cannot fully determine the substantive content of election campaigns. Certain issues force themselves into politics regardless of the parties'

Table 7.1. Party Concepts and Voting Variables

| Party Concept | Relative Impact Expected of | | | |
	Mobilization	Party	Issues	Candidates
Bureaucracy	Low	High	Low	Moderate
Governing caucus	Low	Moderate	High	Low
Cause advocate	High	Low	High	Moderate
Ideological community	High	High	Moderate	Low
Social movement	High	Moderate	High	Low
Urban machine	Moderate	High	Low	High
Office-seeking team	Moderate	Low	High	Moderate
Personal faction	High	Low	Moderate	High

wishes, particularly those based on real-world events, such as economic conditions and war. Current national conditions are always part of the evidence voters use, so parties must devote considerable attention in their campaigns and platforms to praising or belittling the record of the incumbents.

Furthermore, campaign strategies are limited by the conceptual frameworks within which parties operate. All parties must give some attention to each of the four features of mobilization, partisanship, issues, and candidates, but their relative emphases will vary by party type. A social movement must emphasize its vision of the world, even if electorally unpopular, or risk losing its soul, as happened to the American Populists. In contrast, a bureaucratic organization that becomes committed to certain issues may find itself without the tactical flexibility it requires for victory.

VOTING AND PARTY CONCEPTS

The party concepts developed in earlier chapters correspond to expectations of voter behavior. Particular kinds of parties are most likely to thrive when the influences on the voters fit the pattern expected in that party model. In Table 7.1, I make a rough match between these models and the expected impact of each of the electoral variables upon voting behavior.

Each party model is matched with a unique ranking of the voting influences. As abstractions from reality, these influences should be understood in relative, not absolute, terms. These comparisons can be made, first, of the expected relative importance of the different voting influences to each hypothetical party, the horizontal rows of the table. Comparisons can also be made of the relative importance of the different voting influences among the party concepts, the vertical columns of the table. Partisanship, for example, will be taken into account by all varieties of parties, but it will not be of equal priority to each. To the ideological community, given its expressive character, the emotional ties to party will be a particularly important appeal. For the ideal rational office-seeking team, in contrast, the policy inducements offered to utilitarian voters are relatively more important. The voting patterns implied in each model can now be briefly developed. Although abstract, they are not imaginary. Each of the party models, in fact, has been practiced at some time or another in the course of American elections.

The first model, party as bureaucratic organization, assumes voters have a high degree of party loyalty. This type of party is structured to exploit the partisanship of its own membership, but its established routines make it more difficult for it to mobilize new populations. The bureaucratic party uses candidate appeals to supplement its efforts, and issues are subordinated to technique. Van Buren showed the strength of a party bureaucracy in the 1832 presidential election. In his campaign for Jackson, this innovative party leader applied

> the arts of management . . . on a more extensive scale and on a larger stage. He formed committees throughout the Union to sweep up adherents for Jackson and stir the electorate by speaking and writing, in public meetings and private gatherings, glorifying Jackson, replying to the attacks of his opponents, fiercely assailing Adams' administration by a series of concerted movements. The staff required for the performance of this task, and a picked one, was ready to hand— the "politicians." . . . The committees supplied them with the material, popular sentiment offered them a moral base of operations.[7]

With its emphasis on "measures, not men," to take another model, the governing caucus gives even less attention to individual candidates. It hopes for party influence on the vote, but a moderate influence, based on principles. With its view of the electorate as passive spectators, the governing caucus will not stress mobilization.

An earlier presidential election, that of 1800, is illustrative, conducted by parties operating literally as governing caucuses. Republicans met in the national Congress to select Jefferson as their presidential candidate and Aaron Burr as their vice-presidential choice. Although not called a platform, "a clearly defined party program was formulated and repeatedly presented to the electorate." The national party elite also stimulated—and helped to finance—state and local caucuses and campaign organizations. A major effort was made to alter the means of choosing presidential electors, to give the Republicans the advantage of legislative selection on a "winner-take-all" system.

The Republicans, a governing caucus party, successfully contested the election, only to find its new party discipline so strong that Jefferson and Burr were tied in electoral votes for president, requiring selection by the House and ultimately resulting in the Twelfth Amendment to the Constitution. Writing of the contest of 1800, the leading student of the period concludes, "more than any Presidential election that had preceded or would follow for at least a generation, it was a *party* contest for control of the national administration and for determining the direction and management of national policy."[8]

Cause advocates differ from the governing caucus in their efforts to take their programs more directly to the electorate, often because they have been rebuffed within their own party. Consequently, they emphasize partisanship less and issues more and sometimes link their campaign to a prominent candidate. Splinter third parties are illustrative, such as the Free Soil candidacy of Van Buren in 1844. Currently, on the state level, the "Right to Life" party in New York particularly attempts to influence Republican policy on the issue of abortion.

The ideological community and social movement parties are quite different from these first three party models. They are similar to one another in their efforts to change the political world, mobilizing new voters and giving little emphasis to individual leaders. Both regard broad policy issues as important, but the ideological community also stresses firm attachment to the expressive party.

In the United States, ideological communities have been most evident among Marxian parties, which have resembled devout churches as much as electoral organizations. The U.S. Communists, for example, have combined a rhetorical call for mass mobilization with demands for intense devotion from party members. The party's appeal is vividly portrayed by novelist Richard Wright:

It was not the economics of Communism, nor the great power of trade unions, nor the excitement of underground politics that claimed me; my attention was caught by the similarity of the experiences of workers in other lands, by the possibility of uniting scattered but kindred peoples into a whole. It seemed to me that here at last, in the realm of revolutionary expression, Negro experience could find a home, a functioning value and role. Out of the magazines I read came a passionate call for the experiences of the disinherited, and there were none of the lame lispings of the missionary in it. It did not say: "Be like us and we will like you, maybe." It said: "If you possess enough courage to speak out what you are, you will find that you are not alone." It urged life to believe in life.[9]

The Populists exemplify American social movement parties. As Goodwyn describes their character:

This culture was, in the most fundamental meaning of the word, "ideological": it encouraged individuals to have significant aspirations in their own lives, it generated a plan of purpose and a method of mass recruitment, it created its own symbols of politics and democracy in place of inherited hierarchical symbols, and it armed its participants against being intimidated by the corporate culture. The vision and hope embedded in the cooperative crusade held the agrarian ranks together while these things took place and created the autonomous political outlook that was Populism.[10]

The urban machine is a unique party type. It partially mobilizes the electorate, directing its attention to likely supporters, and encourages a strong sense of party loyalty. It cares little about particular issues, but employs the sense of attachment to particular candidates and leaders. Plunkitt colorfully describes this personal attachment:

The politicians who make a lastin' success in politics are the men who are always loyal to their friends, even up to the gate of State prison, if necessary; men who keep their promises and never lie. . . . When the voters elect a man leader, they make a sort of a contract with him. They say, although it ain't written out: "We've put you here to look out for our interests. . . . Be faithful to us, and we'll be faithful to you."[11]

The next party model, the rational team of office seekers, emphasizes voting on the basis of issues, with partisanship significant more as an expression of past issue preferences than in its own right. Particularly conscious of electoral strategy, it may also employ voter mobilization and candidate appeals.

American parties often resemble office-seeking teams. One of many examples is the Democratic party of 1932, which nominated and elected Franklin Roosevelt. FDR first established a strong party ticket through an alliance with Texan John Garner. His subsequent campaign was a model of the rational party, assembling its coalition, promising benefits, and exploiting personal attributes:

> From the beginning of the campaign to the end, Roosevelt kept the initiative, harrying and attacking President Hoover from both the left and the right. His speeches were relatively brief, interesting and dramatic to millions of radio listeners. Ordinarily each dealt with only a single subject. Roosevelt engaged in innumerable meetings with politicians. . . . And there were countless motor cavalcades and whistle-stop gatherings where crowds roared their pleasure at seeing a smiling, confident Roosevelt.

The Democratic campaign of 1932 did deal with significant policy issues, in keeping with the office-seeking model. These issues represented not a coherent ideology, however, but criticisms of the Hoover record and vague promises of future benefits. The Roosevelt team won, but

> the speeches so often veered either right or left and contained so many generalities that to contemporaries it would have been hard to have predicted from them what the New Deal might be. . . . He had received a strong popular mandate and was to make vigorous use of it, but just what that use was to be, beyond the assumption by government of larger responsibilities for the economic welfare of the nation, only the future disclosed.[12]

The personal faction, the last party model, depends on the individual appeal of candidates and attempts to mobilize new voters on their behalf. Issues are important as they are reflected by these candidates, but party loyalty is an impediment to their ambitions. In the 1968 presidential election, Alabama governor George Wallace created a new party that constituted a personal faction. Wallace embodied the resentments of those voters, largely working-class whites, who felt displaced by modernistic trends in the nation, including the civil rights movement, the bureaucratic state, the growth of the service economy, and moral relativism. Asking voters—especially white southern Democrats—to forsake traditional party loyalists, he attempted to mobilize a new coalition of the powerless and the discontented.[13] The personal quality of this coalition was demonstrated when it collapsed after Wallace abandoned the new party, returning to the Democrats in 1972.

AMERICAN VOTERS

Each party model has been partially evident at some point in American history, yet none has been fully and permanently achieved. The extensive empirical literature on American voting behavior delineates this incomplete realization.

Mobilization of American voters is limited, contrary to the expectations of most of the party models. Only about half of the adult population can be certain to vote in a presidential contest, and the proportion is even lower in congressional, state, and local elections. This turnout at the polls is considerably below that of other democracies, where 75–95 percent of the country votes (although these statistical comparisons are somewhat misleading). Furthermore, ballot participation in the United States has decreased in recent decades.[14]

Low turnout in the United States cannot be explained by individual psychological factors alone, such as a lack of knowledge or interest in politics. Although feelings of alienation and inefficacy do reduce voting, their effect is actually quite limited; close to a majority of those claiming to be alienated still vote.[15] The alleged absence of choice between the parties also has no significant effect, for participation is the same among those who do or do not see a difference between Republicans and Democrats.

Political rather than psychological explanations are basic. In requiring personal registration, the American electoral system creates a double burden for voters, unique in the world. Simplification of voting procedures could itself raise turnout by close to 10 percentage points, according to an authoritative analysis. Turning the task of registration over to government, as is common in other democracies, would bring U.S. voting levels close to those of other nations.[16] These legal obstacles have been reinforced by partisan trends, partially accounting for the recent decline in voter participation. Weakened party commitment makes voters less likely to come to the polls, and weakened parties are less likely to bring them.[17] For these reasons, the parties operate in an environment unfavorable to electoral mobilization.

We next turn to the factors that affect the ballot itself, once voters come to the polls.[18] Partisanship is the first because it is the single most important influence on voter behavior. Its impact is consistent with the expectations of most of the party models, which imply either a moderate or even a high influence. In making their choices, voters have a "standing decision" to support their own party, a relationship that has remained consistently evident over the years.[19] Simply put, most persons who consider themselves Democrats will vote for the Democratic candidate for any office, and most Republicans will vote for the Republican nominee.

This party loyalty sometimes has been seen as the reflection of voters' family traditions or their demographic characteristics. In this view, children become Democrats or Republicans much as they usually follow their parents' religion or food tastes. To the limited extent that they act independently, partisanship only mirrors their social class, or religion, or residence, so that "a person thinks, politically, as he is socially."[20]

In reality, partisanship has a more substantial, and a more political, base. Although younger generations tend to maintain the partisan traditions of their parents, the inheritance is considerably attenuated.[21] Particular groups tend to support one party over another, but there are considerable numbers of opposing partisans within every social category. For example, although American union members are more likely to be Democrats than Republicans, the marginal difference is only about 20 percent.[22]

Political views reflect voters' social environment but are more than merely its mirror. Tradition and demography themselves encapsulate political experiences. Since children inherit the social history of their parents, it is sensible, not irrational, that they also inherit the political "faith of the fathers" — and mothers. When children face different circumstances or perceive new party characteristics, however, they may well come to hold different loyalties. Note the insightful testimony of a traditional Irish Democrat, now an ideologically conservative Republican:

> In Washington the older Republicans, the ones over forty-five, looked the way a Hollywood screenwriter would have a Republican

look: Wadsworth Washington III, a man of pinstripes, parentage and pedigree. An older Democrat is a guy named Vito who talks with his hands and wears a lumpy grey suit—he looks like a walking, talking toaster—and represents the wards of Newark.

But with the young it was all changing—and the cliches hadn't caught up! Up on the Hill or at the White House the young rough-looking guy from a state school is probably either a Republican or a conservative, and the snooty sniffy guy with a *Thank You for Not Smoking* sign on his tidy little desk is a Democrat.[23]

Partisanship can be understood as a quick cue, readily available to the voter, a summary of past issue preferences and past loyalties, a means of simplifying the potentially overwhelming complexities of casting a ballot. It identifies a person's loyalties to groups and mates, not only to parties. "Party, for Americans, seems to involve a stable alliance with some people, a shared stance in relation to the state and to the political past. Party, in this sense, presumes we know who we are *with*; it does not imply that we necessarily agree on what *for*."[24]

Party identification in these terms is not simply an emotional attachment (although of course it is also that) but a loyalty based on satisfaction with past results and past associations. This identification is something like the loyalty people feel to their baseball teams or their spouses—held over a long period of sickness and health, sometimes violated in a short dalliance, and subject to permanent change when the original reasons for fidelity disappear.

Voters may, and do, change their basic loyalties, and usually for reasons that are clearly political.[25] The Republican party that fought the Civil War becomes resistant to civil rights, and blacks reverse their traditional partisanship to become the most faithful of Democrats. The Democratic party that elected John Kennedy as president becomes committed to abortion rights, and conservative Catholics leave their historical political home. When a significant number of individuals have changed their loyalties, gradually or suddenly, the total system has undergone a party realignment.[26]

In contemporary times, party loyalty has become both less extensive and less intensive, making partisanship a less definitive influence on the vote. A considerable proportion of the electorate claims to be Independent, identifying with neither of the major parties. Most of these voters do admit to "leaning" toward one or the other of the parties, however, and their behavior is similar to that of avowed partisans.

More significant than change in the extent of partisanship is its decreased intensity. Most Americans continue to identify with the major parties and vote in accord with their professed identifications. Yet they hold these loyalties lightly—more like that of occasional sports fans than of die-hard enthusiasts, more like that of persons in trial "relationships" than of committed spouses. Comparing attitudes toward the Republicans and Democrats over recent decades, Wattenberg found that the "major change that has taken place in the public's evaluations of the parties has been that people feel neutral rather than negative." In place of former passions, "the electorate just no longer has much to say when asked what they like and dislike about the two parties."[27]

With voters willing to subordinate, even change, their party loyalty, partisanship is a real but loose restraint, a tie that still holds but is "frayed," not a fast knot.[28] Other factors become more likely to influence the vote, particularly issue preferences and candidate characteristics. These factors are gaining in their electoral impact, contrary to the implicit expectations of most of the party models.

Issues have both direct and indirect effects on the vote. The indirect effect is their impact on party identification itself, because party loyalties, and changes in these loyalties, can be traced back to some original basis in political issues. As Fiorina aptly resolves a scholarly dispute on these different factors, "Controversies about issue voting versus party identification miss the point: the 'issues' are *in* party identification."[29] Issues, or voters' policy preferences, also have a direct influence of their own on election results. Much of government is obscure to voters, and they often lack the interest or the information to make considered judgments on detailed programs. Within these limitations, however, voters do have preferences and use their ballots to express them.

One overall indicator of these direct effects is the voters' evaluation of the parties' capability in handling "the most important problem facing the nation." Over 90 percent will vote for the party they consider more capable—a suggestion of the connection between issue preferences and the election results.[30] To be sure, this relationship may reflect only a verbal rationalization of a preference actually based on partisanship.[31] Still, we can see the effects of issues (and other influences) independent of partisanship. In all recent presidential elections, for example, a majority of those

Republicans and Democrats dissatisfied with their own party's record crossed party lines to vote for the opposition. Although such discontent is not common, a significant proportion of voters disdain the uncomplaining response, "my party, right or wrong."

What are issues to voters? They are not the same as ideologies, coherent worldviews that lead to consistent attitudes on all particular issues. Although some voters do evidence such coherence or "attitudinal constraint," and the proportion may be increasing, most Americans do not fall neatly into such philosophical categories as "liberal" and "conservative."[32] Political cognition occurs in a variety of ways. Voters use different means to sort out their ideas, some systems resembling ideology and others being less comprehensive.[33]

Voters are concerned with particular items, not worldviews; with inflation and unemployment, not with the merits of capitalism; with U.S. policy toward Russia or Iraq, not with imperialism; with minority employment or abortion, not with theories of social order. At this level, the electorate has been shown to be "moved by concern about central and relevant questions of public policy, of governmental performance, and of executive personality."[34]

These issues not only account for party identification and changes in that identification. On their own, they have substantial influence, leading to the conclusion that "voting decisions are largely motivated by evaluations of where the parties are located on different issues relative to the person's stated position and to a much lesser extent by party identifications unless people are indifferent between the parties on the issues."[35]

Some of the criteria voters employ are *retrospective*, evaluations of the past, such as the record of the party holding control of the White House. For this reason, as conventional political wisdom has it, elections often turn on the level of economic prosperity. Other criteria are *prospective*, preferences about the future course of government. The two kinds of issues, retrospective and prospective, are analytically separate but combined in reality. Knowing the actions that parties have taken in the past, such as their records on economic prosperity and abortion, voters then use that information to judge parties' probable actions in the future.

These "future expectations count and count very heavily among contemporary American voters."[36] Voters use a simple rule: They choose which of the two parties is on their own side of current issues even if they do not share the same intensity on these issues.[37] An advocate of "right-to-choice," for example, will cast her ballot for a like-minded candidate, whether or not that candidate is more or less passionate on the issue.

Candidates are the third and most obvious type of influence on the vote. If nothing else, an election always involves a choice among individuals and always results in some man or woman winning power. Indeed, popular accounts sometimes present elections as only a horse race, no more than a contest among candidates.

Voters are rightly concerned with evaluating individual candidates. A party record, however appealing, is no guarantee that its nominees will carry on its traditions. Attractive issue positions, to be redeemed, require competent, honest, and effective officeholders. Given the complexities of government, the citizenry must entrust its welfare to its leaders, and therefore it must closely examine their trustworthiness.[38]

In considering candidates, voters focus primarily on relevant characteristics. Although there is much speculation about the impact of "candidate images," the voters are not so simpleminded. For the most part, they do not evaluate candidates on "uninformed idiosyncratic responses based on superficial criteria," usually vaguely termed "personality." Instead, voters, and the candidates themselves, emphasize "competence, integrity, and reliability, because they believe these are relevant to the conduct of the office."[39]

Candidates are also evaluated in terms of issues, both their retrospective performance and their future policy promises, elements that predominate in candidate evaluations. Three of five voters now judge the candidates on the basis of their ideology, their positions on individual issues, or the group benefits they promise. This is a decided change since the 1950s when three out of four voters evaluated candidates on no more than their party labels or their individual images.[40]

CHANGING VOTERS AND CHANGING PARTIES

Voters in the United States are affected by all the electoral influences, but their relative importance is now changing. Mobilization of the citizenry is limited, already low by international standards and possibly declining even further. Partisanship has been relatively high, but it is now decreasing in its independent influence. Historically, the impact of issues was low but has grown more significant in recent years. Candidate characteristics, a moderate influence on their own in the past, are coming to have greater weight.

These changes in their total impact constitute a significant transformation of the American electorate, making its behavior less stable and more affected by the events, issues, and politicians of the day. Although partisanship still influences voting greatly, it is a partisanship more consonant with voter policy attitudes than in the past and based less on simple tradition. Issue preferences also affect the vote directly and are an important element in the evaluation of individual candidates. Overall, a decided increase has occurred in the impact of policy considerations in the vote, whether expressed as party image, issue preferences, or candidate evaluations.[41]

The American patterns of voting and contemporary changes have important implications for our party concepts. One basic point is that the character of the American electorate prevents the full realization in practice of any of the party models. Voting in the United States today evidences low mobilization, moderate partisanship, and high impacts of issues and candidate characteristics. A glance back to Table 7.1 shows that this pattern does not fit any of the party models in all respects.

The comparison also shows that the voting pattern does conform to some aspect of virtually every party concept, with the exception of the ideological community model. More specifically, although the fit is not precise, American electoral behavior is particularly consonant with the rather different models of parties as governing caucuses and as office-seeking teams.[42] These similarities suggest the possible direction of American parties.

Ultimately, these parties may fit a new concept of political parties, which we may tentatively call "leadership coalitions." These parties would be centered on and largely directed by the principal public officeholders elected under the party label. In this respect, they would be similar to the office-seeking team but less cohesive. These leaders, given their public responsibilities, will give the parties a clearer policy orientation; they would thereby resemble the governing caucus but with coalitional rather than collective goals. The emerging parties would also share some characteristics of the other models, such as the organizational bureaucracy (but with a mass rather than an elite focus), the social movement (but with coalitional rather than collective goals), and the personal faction (but employing the instrumental rather than the expressive mode).

Current developments in American politics provide some tentative evidence for the emergence of this new kind of party. These include the increased power of legislative leaders in party fund-raising and campaigning, the impact of incumbency on the vote, and the greater cohesion of party members in legislative voting.[43] These are indicators of new party strength but a strength centered on the party's representatives in office, not on its organizational workers. Visible, with high sensitivity to public opinion and in control of vital electoral resources, they may come to define the meaning of American political parties.[44]

The implications of this development for democratic practice can now be only speculative. Parties directed by their visible leadership can facilitate the public's understanding of the choices it faces at the ballot box. Yet such parties may be only collections of individuals, without policy coherence or continuing responsibility for governmental programs.

Future American political parties may be a modern form of the Jeffersonian governing caucus, different in its deeper reach within the electorate. Alternatively, they may be simply the campaigning arms of governmental place-holders and place-seekers. For democracy, the important and unresolved issue is whether citizens will be more than voters. A competitive struggle of elites is certainly a form of popular rule. Yet, in itself, it is hardly a robust exercise of "the consent of the governed."

EIGHT
THE REFORM OF POLITICAL PARTIES

> The regulation of these various and interfering interests forms the principal task
> of modern legislation, and involves the spirit of party and faction in the
> necessary and ordinary operations of the government.
> —*James Madison*[1]

Taking their cue from Madison, Americans have made the regulation of political parties one of the principal tasks of political legislation. In his theory this founding father distrusted parties, yet in his practice he organized the first modern party, the Jeffersonian Republicans. Following Madison, Americans are loyal to their particular parties but do not like them as institutions.

This contradictory attitude may itself account for the frequent concern for party reform, which, Ranney suggests, "has always seemed to many a welcome escape from dilemmas arising from the fundamental ambivalence that has always characterized the attitudes of most Americans toward political parties and political action."[2] Perhaps because voters do not like parties, the United States has devoted a lot of attention to their reform and even to their obliteration.

Reform, however, comprises a multitude of programs, improvements, and sins. Party reformers have favored both greater party control over nominations and leadership selection through direct, popular primaries; increasing financial resources of the parties and limiting their receipts and expenditures; strong party discipline on policy issues and legislative independence; centralized party authority and control at the local grass roots.

The reform programs have varied because they have been based implicitly on different models of political parties. Seeing parties from distinct viewpoints, observers have also evaluated them quite differently. When Edmund Burke, for example, praised political parties, he had in mind the Whigs of his day, who attempted to become a governing caucus, controlling the British House of Commons to achieve a governmental program. A century later, American middle-class mugwump reformers would condemn political parties, exemplified by the urban machine. The differing evaluations followed from the contrasting stances from which Burke and the mugwumps viewed the parties.

Table 8.1. Reform Perspectives of Party Concepts (illustrative method
of selecting presidential nominees)

Goals of Politics: Are/Should Be	Mobilization of Citizens: Is/Should Be	
	Individualist	Majoritarian
Collective	*Progressive*	*Party Government*
	Anti-Machine	Governing caucus
	Cause advocates	Ideological community
		Social movement
	(national primary)	(membership choice)
Coalitional	*Nonpartisanship*	*Party Efficiency*
	Personal faction	Party bureaucracy
		Office-seeking team
	(candidate coalition)	(party convention)

Our discussion of party concepts may illuminate these differences in reform perspectives. In Table 8.1, these concepts are reclassified along two dichotomous dimensions, providing four perspectives on party reform. Both of these dimensions combine descriptions—what politics is said to be about—with normative statements—what politics ought to be.

The first (horizontal) dimension deals with the mobilization of the citizenry. Politics can be seen as individualist, where decisions are or should be made by relatively autonomous persons. Alternatively, politics can be structured toward common action and majoritarian decisions. Generally, reformers who fear parties and wish to restrict their power emphasize individualism, and those who favor party strengthening emphasize more power for democratic majorities.

The second (vertical) dimension is the familiar difference between collective and coalitional goals. Individualists may expect that disaggregated individuals can be brought together on behalf of a common public interest or may simply foresee dispersed coalitions. The difference is also evident among advocates of stronger political parties. Like Burke and Woodrow Wilson, they may look to the achievement of a broad program in the public interest, or, in contrast, they may seek reform only in order to make the parties more effective in promoting the diverse goals of their coalition members.

The combination of these two dimensions results in four perspectives on party reform, labeled in the table, and four quite different programs of specific changes. These different perspectives, illustratively, imply alternative methods for the selection of presidential candidates, as specified in the parentheses within each cell of the table.

From the progressive perspective, a party nominee should be chosen by a national primary open to all voters. Individuals would have direct personal input, leading to a collective national decision. This proposal is actually favored by most Americans in opinion polls.[3]

Another mode of individualist selection, commonly evident today, is through coalitions assembled to support a popular aspirant. Although these coalitions formally operate within a party structure, they are akin to nonpartisan groups. "Rather than depending upon alliances with and commitments from state party organizations . . . candidates for the Presidency are increasingly obliged to mount their search for delegates by building their own personal organizations state by state."[4]

The party government perspective envisages majoritarian action toward the achievement of collective goals. The party's presidential candidate would be selected by the membership, meeting in party caucuses or, alternatively, through a mass plebiscite, as used by the Liberal Democratic party of Great Britain. A focus on party efficiency implies presidential selection through bargaining among party representatives; this was the traditional method, conducted in "smoke-filled rooms" at the quadrennial party conventions.

PROGRESSIVE REFORM

These perspectives differ in their theoretical bases as well as in their policy implications. To some individuals, reform has meant limiting, even eliminating, political parties. Such was the thrust of the Progressive movement in the United States, which led to the most extensive constraints on American political parties.

The general purpose of these reforms was to remove impediments that allegedly obstructed voter control of government and public policy. Wherever possible, direct democracy was to replace institutions of representation. In place of legislative bills, citizens would initiate their own laws and decide on their passage through popular referendums. Officials would be kept on a short leash, subject to frequent election on a long ballot and to recall by a dissatisfied electorate.

As the most conspicuous barrier between the citizenry and the government, parties were a particular target of the Progressives. They were subject to detailed codes of conduct, their finances regulated, their patronage limited through civil service, and their structure prescribed by law. They were treated not as private associations but as "public utilities," to be regulated in the public interest.[5] Along with the new powers of the initiative, referendum, and recall, the taming of political parties would allow the general public interest to escape corruption by special interests and political chicanery.

The most important and enduring Progressive influence on American political parties has been the direct primary, the selection of party nominees through public elections open either to all voters or to those who made a nominal, costless declaration. This Progressive reform was devised as a reaction to the strong urban machines of the day, a sort of "alternate universe." Its origin is openly acknowledged in the rhetoric of its most prominent political patron, Robert LaFollette:

> The direct primary will lower party responsibility. In its stead it establishes individual responsibility. It does lessen allegiance to party and increase individual independence, both as to the public official and as to the private citizen. It takes away the power of the party leader or boss and places the responsibility for control upon the individual.[6]

Ostrogorski, the Progressives' intellectual forefather, believed that enfeebling existing parties would free the individual citizen, and

> will allow, and will even compel him to take a less passive part in the government, to discharge his civic duties in a more conscious way. . . . The citizen will be enabled and obliged to make up his mind on each of the great questions that will divide public opinion. By joining one of the parties which will be formed on this occasion, he will know exactly what he wants, what is the issue, to what he gives his adhesion, where he is going, and how far he will go.[7]

Individual reflection would result, Progressives believed, in the realization of the common interest. In their optimism, they insisted that the true public interest could be located, under the proper circumstances. With Madison the theoretician, they argued that "the public good is disregarded in the conflicts of rival parties" as factions oppose "the permanent and aggregate interests of the community."[8] Unlike Madison's theory and practice, their solution was not to set multiple factions against each other but to remove the impediments of parties and special interests. Debating public principles, right-thinking individuals would then do right.

The direct primary is the principal institutional cause of the American parties' incohesion, or in another view, their openness. It is that rare reform that accomplished its intended aim, the substitution of individualist political action for that of cohesive party majorities. The institutionalization of primaries has meant that "organizational leaders and activists often can do no more than exert influence over nominations. . . . It bolsters individual representation of a kind always encouraged by the electoral separation of legislative and executive branches. Elected officials are expected to respond to their constituencies and not merely to parties whose labels they carry."[9]

The individualist focus of progressivism continues to the present and forms the theoretical basis of a series of decisions of the U.S. Supreme Court, dealing with another aspect of parties, political patronage. Virtually outlawing the use of patronage for appointive positions, the Court in 1990 prohibited party tests even in hirings and promotions. Although giving little attention to parties directly, Justice William Brennan asserted, with scant evidence, that "political parties are nurtured by other, less intrusive and equally effective means" and that they "have already survived the substantial decline in patronage employment practices in this century."[10]

Speaking for a 5–4 majority, Brennan instead based his decision on the individualistic First Amendment, which bars the government "from wielding its power to interfere with its employees' freedom to believe and associate, or to not believe and not associate." Rewarding party workers, or assuring that loyalists staffed government jobs, was found to be insufficient grounds for patronage, which, according to the Court majority, "decidedly impairs the elective process by discouraging free political expression by public employees."[11]

In dissent, Justice Antonin Scalia presented a fulsome endorsement of political parties generally and of patronage particularly. He began with the wry observation that the judicial ban on patronage "will be enforced by a corps of judges (the members of this Court included) who overwhelmingly owe their office to its violation. Something must be wrong here," declared Scalia, "and I suggest it is the Court."[12] More supportive of patronage than most political scientists, Scalia argued that it protects government from "the demands of small and cohesive interest groups," stimulates most of "the local political activity supporting parties," enforces party discipline and furthers party success, promotes the "social and political integration of excluded groups," and facilitates moderate and effective public policy. Without patronage, parties might survive, he warned, not as "the forges upon which many of the essential compromises of American politics are hammered out" but as no more than "convenient vehicles for the conducting of national presidential elections."[13] His minority opinion is an articulate, but rare, official defense of parties against dominant progressive thought.

NONPARTISANSHIP

A second variety of reform, nonpartisanship, is even more hostile to political parties. Progressives usually accept parties as inevitable even if evil, but nonpartisan advocates seek to eliminate them completely. Agreeing with progressives that individual decisions should be foremost in politics, they are less certain that the process will result in a clearly collective policy.

The most common form of nonpartisanship is essentially an abandonment of politics in favor of expert, technical rule, its rhetorical premise being that "there is no Republican or Democratic way to clean the streets." Policy questions can be resolved by objective standards and implemented by expert administrators. These views have been most evident in municipal government, resulting in nonpartisan elections and the establishment of city-manager governments in place of elected chief administrators in the vast majority of local jurisdictions.[14]

A similar concept of government as impartial administration underlies legislation limiting partisan activity by civil servants or prohibiting major public officials from holding party offices.[15] Such prohibitions actually violate the logic of *Rutan* in its emphasis on the individual political freedom of officeholders. Still, nonpartisanship has considerable support among American voters, with substantial proportions now close to a majority ready to abandon party labels even for state or national elections.[16]

The emphasis of nonpartisanship on efficiency disguises but does not eliminate political conflict. In reality, there can be party differences even on apparently mundane administrative matters. Whose streets are cleaned, or whether money is spent on streets or on schools, or who controls the sanitation department are political questions, not matters of scientific determination. More generally, winners and losers are different under nonpartisanship, which tends—especially when combined with at-large electoral systems—to favor the interests of those with higher income and social status.[17] In such circumstances, there is a "lessened responsiveness of cities to the enduring conflicts of political life."[18]

In practice, nonpartisanship substitutes a more personal politics for party competition. Ford predicts this development in his attack on such reforms, and his comments, although directed specifically at primaries, are even more apposite to nonpartisanship. These reforms would certainly transform politics, he argues, but not in the direction its proponents hoped. Instead, parties would change, in our terms, from bureaucracies to personal factions:

> The direct primary may take advantage and opportunity from one set of politicians and confer them upon another set, but politicians there will always be so long as there is politics. The only thing that is open to control is the sort of politicians we shall have. . . . Its pretense of giving power to the people is a mockery. The reality is that it scrambles power among faction chiefs and their bands, while the people are despoiled and oppressed. . . . The practical effect will be to substitute for existing boss rule a far more corrupt, degraded and imperious sort of boss rule.[19]

The overall effect of nonpartisan reform has been to shift responsibility for political action from coalitions assembled within parties to individual leaders. Under nonpartisanship, politics comes to resemble the "bastard feudalism" of the late Middle Ages, when personal allegiance to a powerful baron became the road to power, and the party becomes no more than "a political kingdom to be disputed by private armies owing their allegiance not to some local machine, but to a nationally puissant family or individual."[20]

The nonpartisan variety of reform has also been evident in legislation on campaign finance, such as the 1974 federal election law. The basic thrust of this legislation has been to provide money for individual candidates rather than for parties. Federal funds subsidize the campaigns of presidential hopefuls and then pay all the expenses of those who capture the Republican and Democratic designations. The expectation, and the reality, is that most contributions will go to candidates and not to parties, and the parties themselves are restricted in the support they can give to candidates running under their banner.

The law does provide some limited support for parties, since the cost of their national conventions is paid by the government and larger personal contributions are allowed to parties than to individual candidates. Moreover, the national parties have found loopholes in the law that magnify their financial impact. Still, the basic thrust of the finance laws has been to emphasize personal politics rather than partisan politics.[21]

This individualist character was underlined by the Supreme Court when it reviewed the federal election finance laws.[22] Candidates could not be restricted in spending their own money, nor could interest groups supporting a candidate if they operated "independently." Given the high costs of politics, the Court declared, "A restriction on the amount of money a person or group can spend on political communication during a campaign necessarily reduces the quantity of expression" and therefore unconstitutionally establishes "substantial . . . restraints on the quantity and diversity of political speech."[23]

Turning from contributions to expenditures, the Court ruled that candidates could not be compelled to limit their spending, even though such limitations might make an election contest more equal. A ceiling on expenditures could only be accomplished if voluntarily accepted by a candidate in exchange for federal funds. In contrast, limits on political party spending were not challenged.

The logical inference from the Court's decision is that corruption is a selective disease. Parties are so liable to infection that they must be quarantined. Individual candidates, on the other hand, can be immunized. They can spend freely, or they can be bribed by governmental election funds to restrict their expenditures, all without risk to the health of the electoral process. As long as contributions from any one donor are limited, they will not cause an epidemic of political illness. In the nonpartisan diagnosis, parties carry disease, but money itself is free of germs.

PARTY GOVERNMENT

The most debated reforms, at least among academics, have been those directed toward achieving party government. In the United States, the most prominent of these proposals, dating from 1950, is based on the governing caucus model, as discussed in chapter 3.[24] Other models share its perspective in seeking to make parties the vehicles of cohesive majorities promoting a common policy program.

To achieve some approximation of party government, its advocates have urged greater emphasis on policy declarations within the party, tighter party discipline in Congress, and greater membership involvement. The party government model is supported by large proportions of party leaders. Its advocates include a majority of Republican national convention delegates, national committee members, and county chairs and about one-third of the corresponding Democratic groups.[25]

Many of the specific changes urged by these advocates have been achieved in the forty years of American intellectual discussion of the party government model. The parties show considerable ideological agreement now among their activists and increased coherence in congressional voting, and this trend toward greater programmatic unity is mirrored among their mass voting supporters. The Democratic party for a time also experimented with midterm conferences, devoted to the elaboration of party programs.

Within Congress, active party caucuses now debate party programs, the traditional seniority system has been modified, and a modicum of discipline has been applied to assure loyalty to party programs by committee chairs. The parties' membership bases also have been broadened. Tens of millions of individuals now participate in choosing the party's presidential nominee, millions contribute money, tens of thousands come to open party caucuses.

However, party government does not exist today in the United States. Major policy innovations do occur but not because one of the parties develops a program, receives popular endorsement for its proposal, and then enacts its platform. Instead, the nation now has a "kind of government by ad-hoc coalition that has left many politicians in both parties confused about when to clash and when to cooperate," resulting in "a muddling of the traditional distinctions between Democrats and Republicans."[26]

The difficulties in achieving party government are partly institutional, rooted in the Constitution. The separation of powers, federalism, fixed terms of election, and the ultimate dependence of legislators on constituency approval have always deterred realization of the party government model. These fundamental limits have been reinforced by what John White calls "the allure of divided government," the voters' preference for opposing party control of the presidency and the Congress. No longer an aberration, partisan division has become characteristic of American politics.[27]

A deeper problem with the party government model is theoretical, for its advocates have been unclear in their ultimate aims. There is some truth in the criticism that these advocates have really hoped that the American system of separated institutions might be replaced by a Westminster, British-style parliamentary system.[28] Some party government advocates have urged this change, some have championed partial steps toward this goal, such as coterminous terms for Congress and the president, and some have expressed "admiration" for British-style government though admitting it is not feasible in the United States.[29] Without a clear objective, the case for party government has weakened intellectually.

Furthermore the advocates of party government are uncertain of their basic concept of party. The classic report of the American Political Science Association, for example, urged a programmatic emphasis characteristic of a governing caucus, active local parties reminiscent of an ideological community, and party centralization more akin to a party bureaucracy.[30] Efforts toward party government are particularly confused in regard to the roles of the mass membership and of the mass electorate within the party.

The critical arguments among those taking the party government perspective are implicitly based on different theories of representation, best analyzed by Pitkin.[31] Party leadership has very different meanings, depending on the basis of power within the party. In a theory of "descriptive representation," leaders are expected to be no more than a mirror of party members, simply reflecting their descriptive characteristics or their candidate preferences. Such representation is more suitable to the progressive or the nonpartisan perspectives on party reform.

In more vigorous modes of representation, leaders will also act on behalf of party members, either as accountable agents of rank-and-file views or as trustees authorized to function in their place. These different concepts of representation are closely related to the different concepts of party and lead to different proposals for party change.

Seeing the party as a social movement implies descriptive representation, based on the party's mass support. This premise leads to demographic quotas within party bodies, with power allocated among such groups as women, racial minorities, or young people in proportion to their numbers in the electorate. The same premise underlies proportional representation of candidate preferences in the national conventions.

Seeing the party as an ideological community implies representation as agency, with leaders obligated to support the distinctive policy program of the party. This aim can be accomplished best through open party assemblies that will attract issue enthusiasts. Seeing the party as a governing caucus implies representation as authorization, permitting discretion in policy choices by leaders. This goal leads to enhanced power for those in formal positions of party and public office.

Recent party reforms have demonstrated these conceptual confusions and uncertain aims. In the same documents, reformers have favored both greater power for the party center and more power for local party caucuses, both greater control over leadership by party activists and selection of leadership in primaries open to all voters who effortlessly ask for the party's nominating ballot, both representation within the party for designated demographic groups and representation on the basis of candidate preferences.[32]

As Ranney recounted the debates in the first Democratic party reform commission, "We contended that requiring representation of biological characteristics was at odds with the commission's other objectives of open access and representation of preferences. The party could provide for a fair fight or it could provide for a guaranteed result, we said, but it could not provide for both."[33] Indeed, the only consistency in these reform programs has been hostility to state party groups, if not to all regular organizations. Party government reform is difficult enough to achieve in American conditions; it will be impossible without theoretical clarity and without attention to the parties themselves.

PARTY EFFICIENCY

A fourth group of party reformers seeks to make the parties stronger and more efficient electoral competitors. Their doctrine could be termed one of party responsibility, in two senses: The parties should be responsible for their own internal affairs; given such autonomy, they can be held responsible by the electorate for their conduct of government. These changes would make parties more akin to our models of the party bureacracy and the office-seeking team.

Although the terms are often confused, party responsibility reform is less ambitious than party government reform since it does not insist that the parties have coherent policy programs or pursue collective goals. The party is seen as a coalition, often self-interested, but one that can still be an instrument for popular control through the electorate's judgements on its past record and future promises. In this perspective, a party's most important contribution is in "establishing accountability to the enduring values of a democratic society in elites that gain power in systems of mass persuasion."[34]

Reform toward party efficiency has first taken a route toward deregulation, or removing legal restrictions on the parties. As we have seen, control of parties was part of the Progressive movement. This effort was supplemented by court decisions, which upheld legislative restrictions and added judicial limits on the conduct of party primaries. Recent landmark decisions by the U.S. Supreme Court have reversed the course of regulation.

Primaries came before the Court in challenges to the exclusion of blacks from southern Democratic parties during the era of legal segregation. For some years, the Court concentrated on the connections between party action and state action. At first, it found racial exclusion from primaries unconstitutional, because the parties were acting as "the organs of the State itself, the repositories of official power" and therefore were subject to the restaints of the Fourteenth Amendment. [35]

State laws regulating primaries were then amended to leave participation in primaries and racial discrimination to the discretion of the parties themselves. The Court briefly accepted this legal maneuver. Recognizing the party as a private association the Court underlined "the right of the party to exist, to define its membership, and to adopt such policies as to it shall seem wise." [36]

Soon after, the Court shifted ground. No longer viewing parties as state agencies, it still found the "white primary" unconstitutional under the Fifteenth Amendment, the guarantee of racial equality in elections. Because primaries are an intrinsic element in the electoral process, wrote the Court, they are subject to the constitutional "right to participate in the choice of elected officials without restriction by any state because of race." Moreover, a state cannot even permit "a private organization to practice racial discrimination in the election. Constitutional rights would be of little value if they could be thus indirectly denied." [37]

As Kester summarizes, these decisions provide "no support for any loose generalizations that action by a political party is 'state action' . . . but rather [focus] on identifying what is an 'election' in which article I and the fifteenth amendment confer a federal constitutional right to vote." [38] Ultimately, this series of cases, although preventing racial discrimination in a public election, left parties considerable freedom in other, nonracial, respects.

These associational rights of political parties have recently won strong endorsement from the Court. As the parties changed their nominating procedures in the 1970s, a series of court cases increased their power, even in opposition to state law. The parties were allowed to set their own convention rules, to unseat delegates who had been duly elected under state statutes, and contrary to state law, to mandate either the selection of delegates in closed caucuses or to open their primaries to self-declared Independents.[39]

The most expansive Court endorsement of party freedom came in 1989 in a successful challenge to California's detailed legislation on political parties. The Court struck down the state's ban on party endorsement of candidates in primaries and overturned extensive state regulation that "limits a political party's discretion in how to organize itself, conduct its affairs, and select its leaders." These regulations were found to "violate the free speech and associational rights of political parties and their members guaranteed by the First and Fourteenth Amendments."[40]

The second aspect of party efficiency reform is to strengthen the parties directly, a process of party renewal to make them more efficient bureaucracies and more capable office-seeking teams. The national parties have become well-developed institutions, symbolized by the construction of permanent headquarters in Washington.[41] Using their now considerable funds, the parties also provide extensive services to candidates. In the Democratic party, the nominating process has been repeatedly "re-reformed" to increase the role of party leaders and elected officials.[42]

Recent amendments to the federal campaign-finance laws are modest steps in this strengthening process allowing larger contributions to parties than to candidates, freeing state parties to spend money on behalf of federal candidates, and increasing the federal subsidy to parties implicit in payment of the cost of national nominating conventions. The parties have also increased their financial impact. The national party committees now receive legally unlimited but controversial "soft money" contributions for their organizational or noncampaign activities.[43] They also act as conduits for contributions by political action committees, which they "bundle" together and then forward to favored candidates.

Further steps toward greater party efficiency were suggested by a self-appointed Commission on National Elections, in preparation for the 1988 presidential election. On the premise that election reform "should begin by seeking to strengthen the role of the political parties," the group urged that parties become more central in the national contest, particularly by taking over the management of televised debates between the presidential candidates, replacing the previous sponsors, the nonpartisan League of Women Voters.[44]

Although the national parties did sponsor one of the two television

debates in 1988, the action was itself controversial and provided little reason to believe that further steps toward strengthened parties would gain
wide support. Indeed the commission itself, though favorable to stronger
parties, shied away from more thoroughgoing proposals, such as redirect-
ing campaign contributions from candidates to parties, direct subsidies to
the parties, or restrictions on presidential primaries.

The same reluctance is evident in congressional debates on amendment
of campaign-finance statutes. Although there is widespread agreement that
present laws carry the potential for corruption, proposed revisions have
centered on limiting the financial impact of political action committees and
restrictions on "soft money." The emphasis has been on aiding individual
congressional candidates rather than on increasing the parties' role.

Support of the parties would require either major relaxation of the limits
on party contributions or direct public subsidies. Each course has its proponents, but Democrats would probably benefit more from public subsidies
and Republicans from greater party autonomy in campaign finance. The
partisan conflict has led to stalemate, not party renewal.

Such hesitancy illustrates the obstacles challenging even marginal steps
toward party renewal. Timid change, however, will not alter fundamental problems. The current deficiencies of American parties, Reiter convincingly
argues, result from long-term trends and hostilities, originating in Progressive
legislation and the direct primary and then reinforced by irreversible innovations in technology and campaign methods.[45] Recent changes in party rules
and legislation have probably magnified the effects of these more fundamental
causes, as some contend.[46] Other commentators dispute this conclusion,
seeing the parties as recently strengthened through mobilization of new groups
and organizational development.[47]

To the extent that party flaccidity is due to deliberate design or to unintended
consequences of rules and legislation, these effects can be reversed by new
party and legislative decisions. Such actions are already under way, as we have
seen in judicial decisions, finance legislation, and modification of national
nominating procedures. The character of American parties, however, ultimately depends on the values Americans apply to politics.

PARTY REFORM AND DEMOCRATIC VALUES

Strong or weak parties reflect not so much the nation's view of parties alone
but its more basic attitudes toward politics and government. In reforming

parties, we must first ask what we expect from government. The answers will probably lead us to emphasize one or another of the perspectives on party reform.

In setting reform goals for government, we could make a fundamental choice for rapid and programmatically coherent action. Reform would then be viewed from the perspective of party government. Alternatively, we may prefer consensual action, slower but more consistent over time. In this case, the individualist programs of the progressive or the nonpartisan perspectives are more appropriate. The party efficiency perspective, depending on circumstances, permits both alternatives.

We must also ask what we expect for ourselves and from others. If we want to maximize our individual preferences, parties may be a hindrance; individuals can express their particular ideas better when they are less constrained by the opinions and pressures of others. If the facts of modern life make self-sufficiency impossible, we may still strive for personal influence through individual contacts with officials or in the unmediated politics of direct democracy. These are the goals of reform from the progressive and nonpartisan perspectives.

These political values may be psychologically satisfying to each individual but at the same time frustrating because little effective action can be achieved. From the reform perspectives of party government and party efficiency, the force of majoritarian action can unite individuals into effective combinations. Coalitional or collective goals then replace personal access to government, as increased power is bought in the coin of individual preferences. Substituting for the Anti-Federalists' "rough fellowship of the deliberative community," these parties "draw us toward public goals even when interest and ideology pull in opposite directions."[48]

These conflicts in values are congenial to Americans, who live under a Constitution designed to create a government both strong and trammeled. In the debate on party reform, these same ambivalences are evident. Americans want parties to offer distinctive choices, yet they disdain partisan conflict. They cherish their individual expression yet seek effective collective action from their partisan officials. They want to divorce government from politics but demand that parties take a stand and act on the issues.

Americans view parties both ambiguously and ambivalently. Sometimes they are evaluated and accepted as instruments of democracy but are also criticized and regulated when they become too efficient in their pursuit of power. At other times they are expected to be expressive models of internal democracy, and then they are disparaged when they fall short of this standard. Especially troublesome is the possible conflict between these goals, the possibility that parties can be either efficient or democratic but not both. The nation has been loath to agree with Schattschneider that "democracy is not to be found *in* the parties but *between* the parties."[49]

To explore these questions more fully, we must relate parties to more general democratic theory. As the review of perspectives on party reform suggests, democratic goals are not necessarily consistent; indeed, they may be inherently contradictory but still attractive. To understand American democracy, we will need to join in Whitman's American boast,

> Do I contradict myself?
> Very well then I contradict myself,
> (I am large, I contain multitudes.)[50]

NINE

COMMON IMPULSES: POLITICAL PARTIES
AND AMERICAN DEMOCRACY

In politics, as in life, the desired best can be the enemy of the attainable good. Political parties are not ideal groups, but for democracy they are "good enough."

Parties have been shunned by political theorists, even by some advocates of democracy. They are seen as threats to the overriding needs of the nation or to vital group interests or as entities capable of undermining the will of a united populace. Yet parties continue to exist and even occasionally to earn praise for their necessary role in promoting the practice, if not always in satisfying the ideals, of democracy.

Parties are defended, and defensible, because they provide an effective way to balance conflicting philosophical values, to deal with political realities, to close the gap between society's reach and its grasp. American parties combine two different strains of democratic political theory, liberal and communitarian, I argue, and contribute to partial realization of democratic values. Current trends in American politics underline these contributions, leading to my concluding recommendations for party reconstruction in the United States.

THE UNCERTAIN PLACE OF PARTIES

Opposition to political parties is long-standing. In eighteenth-century England, Henry Bolingbroke attacked the emerging parliamentary caucuses, arguing against these advocates of special interests, and for the power of a "patriot king," who would unselfishly pursue the national good:

> Instead of abetting the divisions of his people, he will endeavour to unite them, and to be himself the centre of their union: instead of putting himself at the head of one party in order to govern his people, he will put himself at the head of his people in order to govern, or more properly to subdue, all parties.[1]

Despite such opposition, parties did develop, particularly vigorously in the United States, but attacks also expanded. By the late nineteenth century, Ostrogorski expressed a common opinion of reformers that parties, selfishly and inevitably, neglected the common good, for "it is as idle as it is absurd to entrust, even in part, the custody of the general interest to private interests. . . . There is no possible *condominium* in the public sphere."[2]

The progressive and nonpartisan perspectives on party reform convey this hostile tradition. The antiparty attitude continues among contemporary Americans, who are prone to agree that "our system of government would work a lot more efficiently if we could get rid of conflicts between the parties altogether" and that "the parties more often than not create conflicts where none really exists."[3]

Suspicion of parties comes from three very different sources: statist, democratist, and liberal. Daadler points to two of these grounds. The first is a statist tradition in which "the state was widely regarded as an instrument of a higher moral order. Its sovereignty was to be protected from the encroachment of special interest." Second is a "democratist" tradition, as in "Rousseau's desire to safeguard the direct expression of popular will from representation and interference" by partial associations.[4]

The statist tradition opposes not only competitive political parties but democracy itself. Pursuing the ideal public good, statists disdain the "petty" interests incorporated within parties. To achieve the public good requires the wisdom and vision of leaders with special, inculcated traits rather than persons who will follow the inherently limited wishes of a mass populace. To achieve justice, Plato's goal, a king must also be a philosopher, instructed over decades, who works reluctantly to achieve the public's needs while disregarding its mistaken wants.

In a less benevolent form, statism is also expressed by totalitarian leaders. Using their monopolistic political party to arouse popular feeling, they disdain the competition between parties as evidence of bourgeois decadence. In Mussolini's words, "Fascism conceives of the State as an absolute, in comparison with which all individuals or groups are relative, only to be conceived of in their relation to the State."[5] Instead of election through parties, the popular will is expressed by the leader, such as Hitler, who personally embodies the will of the nation, or by the party, as in a Leninist government.

The democratist tradition also sees parties as deficient, but for a different reason. The statist critics believe parties allow too much popular control over government; the extreme democrats see parties as too restrictive of the citizenry. Only direct rule by the people, and their personal involvement in all principal decisions, is legitimate. Progressive devices such as the referendum and initiative are modern manifestations of this belief. The theoretical foundation is best expressed by Rousseau: "Sovereignty, being nothing less than the exercise of the general will, can never be alienated and . . . the Sovereign, who is no less than a collective being, cannot be represented except by himself."[6]

Legitimate democratic government to Rousseau is literally self-government, best demonstrated in cities and small states. Without such direct participation government is illegitimate, for "every law that the people has not ratified in person is null and void—is, in fact, not a law." Parties are also illegitimate, for they usurp the people's inalienable power; therefore, "The people of England regards itself as free: but it is grossly mistaken: it is free only during the election of members of parliament."[7]

A third source of opposition flows from a liberal tradition, which sees strong parties as threats to vital social interests. Madison, though admitting that factions were inevitable in a free society, still complained that "the public good is disregarded in the conflicts of rival parties, and that measures are too often decided, not according to the rules of justice and the rights of the minor party, but by the superior force of an interested and overbearing majority."[8] Madison developed his quintessential American political theory to control and enfeeble factions and parties, the dangerous expressions of political power.

In the spirit of Madison, even the most successful American politicians, the presidents, have been embarrassed by parties and prone to wish them gone. George Washington set the tone in his Farewell Address, denouncing the "baneful effects of the Spirit of Party," which "make the public administration the mirror of the ill-concerted and incongruous projects of faction, rather than the organ of consistent and wholesome plans digested by common councils, and modified by mutual interests."[9]

Presidential inaugural addresses, perhaps the most important civic ritual of the United States, maintain Washington's antipartisanship. Fresh from a partisan triumph, the new chief executive will proclaim with John Kennedy that "we observe today not a victory of party, but a celebration of freedom" or with George Bush declare, "The American people await action. They didn't send us here to bicker. They ask us to rise above the merely partisan."[10] Only Woodrow Wilson drew the obvious connection between his party and his new power as president.

In their actions as well as in their speeches, presidents have disdained parties. Jefferson, the first elected partisan, worked "to obliterate the traces of party and consolidate the nation." Franklin Roosevelt, the triumphant leader of a new Democratic majority, made overtures to his 1940 Republican opponent to form a new movement. Dwight Eisenhower speculated on the possibility of consolidating Republicans and Democrats into a common moderate party.[11]

Defenders of political parties, fewer in number, are often apologetic. Bryce did not praise parties but found them acceptable means to manage and pacify the newly enfranchised democratic masses. The justification for parties is that voters tend to be "so indifferent, or so ignorant, that it is necessary to rouse them, to drill them, to bring them up to vote." Still, he worried, party activity "carries the community still further from the democratic ideal. . . . If it is impossible to arrest the development of party organizations, what can be done to check their incidental evils?"[12]

Similarly, Ford found parties necessary because the "mass of the people will quite properly hold that they have more important things to attend to than electioneering. They will leave that to those to whom it offers rewards." Politics was properly left to specialists, who were given responsibility and then held accountable.[13] Interestingly, Ostrogorski drew a similar connection between the deficiencies of voters and the strength of parties, which "raised political indifferentism to the level of a virtue."[14]

POLITICAL PARTIES AND DEMOCRATIC PRACTICE

The role of parties in democracy appears to be only grudgingly conceded. If voters would simply fit the prescriptions of the "democratic ideal," parties could be discarded. They are humanity's punishment for preferring the apples of personal interests to the Eden of benevolent leadership in a harmonious community. To appreciate parties more positively, we need to examine the differing concepts of democracy.

We have considered three dimensions of democratic theory: autonomous or accessible leadership, collective or coalitional voter goals, and limited or extensive participation. Each of these dimensions must be examined when constructing democracy, yet each carries a dilemma. Autonomy allows leadership to pursue a vision of the public good, but that leadership may sacrifice its populace to its vision. Keeping leaders accessible limits that danger but introduces the opposite problem, that leaders may be so subject to public opinion that they neglect long-term problems for immediate popularity. In such a case, officials "do not develop the will to lead, nor a firm sense of responsibility for leadership."[15]

Democratic politics attempts to reconcile the needs of any society for effective government with a distinctive objective, popular determination of the leaders and policies of government. To some political thinkers, the two goals have seemed inherently incompatible. Choosing leaders by popular ballot was akin to asking a blind man to select colors, said George Mason.[16] Asking the common herd to select policy was as foolish, Plato believed, as asking rude sailors rather than expert pilots to steer a ship safely through a stormy sea. But without popular control, leaders may steer their ship onto an inhospitable beach that they regard as the site of a personal utopia. As Mill warns, "Rulers and ruling classes are under a necessity of considering the interests of those who have the suffrage; but of those who are excluded, it is in their option whether they will do so or not."[17]

Another dilemma concerns the goals of voters. Some goals in politics are truly collective—clean air, for example—and an effective democracy must go beyond the particular interests involved in pure coalitional politics. Individuals, however, are more prone to consider their individual goals and those of their coalition partners and to leave others to worry about collective goods.[18] Furthermore, even the most evident collective goals cannot be achieved without costs to some people more than to others. A society that neglects these individual interests in pursuit of collective goods will harm some people—displaced workers in polluting industries, for example.

Although highly valued in democracy, participation also presents problems. To arouse extensive participation, emotions must be enlisted, but these emotions may be turned toward intolerance and violence. Even when these dangers are avoided, an emphasis on participation faces the enduring problem that because of the multiple demands on citizens, many of which are more pressing than politics, participation is likely to be sporadic, at least partially uninformed, and unrepresentative in character. In practice, democracy will evidence only limited participation. In the conditions of modern mass society, that course is often a rational choice for individuals facing numerous demands on their limited time.

Through political parties, democracies may achieve reasonable balances between the dichotomies of these three dimensions. Parties make leaders accessible to the mass citizenry; elections provide the formal means, but accessibility is realized only when parties organize competition at the polls. At the same time, because party loyalty assures them of a regular basis of support, leaders have a measure of discretion in the determination of public policy. Parties are a principal component of social pluralism that "supports liberal democracy by providing social bases of free and open competition for leadership, widespread participation in the selection of leaders, restraint in the application of pressures on leaders, and self-government in wide areas of social life."[19]

Parties may also meld collective and coalitional goals. By combining the interests of individuals, they aggregate particular wants into more general programs; when sufficiently generalized, the programmatic cause of the party may displace these particular interests. The effects are illustrated by Burke's promotion of party as a unified principled group or by Van Buren's subordination of personal goals to party interests. As Tocqueville suggests, "As soon as a man begins to treat of public affairs in public, he begins to perceive that he is not so independent of his fellow-men as he had at first imagined. . . . The electoral system brings a multitude of citizens permanently together, who would otherwise always have remained unknown to each other."[20]

Parties deal especially with the problems of democratic participation. For their own electoral purposes they encourage mass participation, but they also guide it. Mass involvement is directed toward specific purposes, most obviously party victory. At the same time, participants learn something about the claims and needs of other party allegiants and about the complexities of public policy.

POLITICAL PARTIES AND DEMOCRATIC VALUES

These dimensions of political parties imply different political values. Any model of a political party encapsulates a combination of individual and social preferences. On an individual level, Dahl has suggested "three criteria for authority."[21] Ideally, individuals would want government to maximize their personal choice, maximize competence in the conduct of public affairs, and maximize economy in the use of their own limited resources, such as time. These criteria parallel our own dimensions, respectively, of voters' goals, leadership, and participation.

The problem, Dahl shows, is that these goals of government cannot be maximized simultaneously so long as there are contending groups in society. If individuals continually work to achieve their personal choice from government or to locate competent leaders, they do so at the cost of economy of time. If competent leaders can be found, they may make decisions different from a particular voter's preferences. In dealing with real governments, citizens must accept some compromise in combining these goals.

Political parties affect the achievement of these various goals. Applying Dahl's criteria, parties clearly promote economy by providing simple cues for voters. Indeed, critics such as Ostrogorski complain that parties provide these cues too readily, allowing voters to neglect their duty as citizens.

Achieving competence is less certain through political parties, depending on whether the recruitment standards used by parties match those needed in government. Traditional presidential nominating procedures, for example, were once said to exclude "great men," just as modern reforms in the system are said to handicap effective presidential government.[22] Achieving personal choice, the third criterion, is also uncertain through parties. By uniting with others, some voters may gain some of their preferences but at the cost of surrendering or compromising other objectives.

Beyond individual preferences, a political system also incorporates more general social values. Democratic political theorists, Alan Ware shows, have emphasized three values, which he terms "interest optimalization, the exercise of control, and civic orientation."[23]

According to the first value, democracy should strive for public policies demanded by the populace, in Bentham's words, seeking "the greatest happiness of the greatest number." A second justification for democracy is that it enables the citizenry to control their government and even "to remove or alter the legislative, when they find the legislative act contrary to the trust reposed in them."[24] The third democratic value is more expansive, stressing personal development. To John Stuart Mill, democratic institutions are desirable insofar as "they tend to foster in the members of the community the various desirable qualities ... moral, intellectual, and active."[25]

These goals are not necessarily contradictory, yet they are not easily reconciled. The first goal deals with substantive results, the second focuses on procedure, the third on individual psychology. Moreover, no necessary relationship exists among them. Achieving the optimal resolution of interests, for example, does not necessarily imply either the exercise of control or the development of a civic orientation, unless we assume tautologically

Table 9.1. Party Concepts and Priorities of Democratic Values

Preference for Civic Orientation	Relative Preference for	
	Interest Optimization	Exercise of Control
Higher preference	Social movement Ideological community	Urban machine
Lower preference	Governing caucus Cause advocate Office-seeking team	Personal faction Bureaucractic organization

that decisions made by democratic controllers or participants are inevitably correct. Indeed, much of political philosophy, beginning with Plato, argues that democratic decisions are likely to be wrong and that democratic participation is to be feared, not welcomed.

Furthermore, the goals of exercising control and civic orientation are quite different and may even be contradictory in some instances. To further civic development, for example, we might enlarge the size of legislative chambers. The result would be that the exercise of control would be less effective, as the size of the body becomes unwieldy, most individuals will be unable to speak, and action will be virtually impossible.

In exercising control, the electorate intervenes, but only in limited ways and on specified occasions: "There is government *for* the people; there is no government *by* the people."[26] In contrast, an electorate with a true civic orientation will participate broadly and regularly, fitting Tocqueville's description of the nineteenth-century American: "He takes a lesson in the form of government from governing. The great work of society is ever going on before his eyes and, as it were, under his hands."[27]

Parties may promote some but not necessarily all of these democratic objectives. Each of the different party models developed in this book emphasizes some of these values and gives lesser attention to others. The relative importance of each of the three values in the various party models is suggested in Table 9.1.

Two kinds of comparison are included in the table. In the horizontal rows, the relative importance of the values of interest optimization and the exercise of control are compared. In the vertical columns, the comparison is of either of these to the third value, civic orientation. (The results of these latter comparisons are identical.) Illustratively, the concept of party as a social movement connotes a theory of democracy as the achievement of particular policy interests rather than the exercise of control. This concept gives a still greater priority to the development of the citizenry, however.

There is some relationship, although incomplete, between these values and the previous dimensions of democracy. On the dimension of leadership, democracy is somewhat more likely to be defined as the exercise of control among the models that see leadership as autonomous rather than as accessible. On the dimension of voter goals, interest optimization is stressed among the models that seek collective rather than coalitional goals. On the dimension of participation, civic orientation is more likely to be emphasized among the models that pursue extensive rather than limited participation.

Each of the party models promotes some values of democracy but slights others. Party bureaucracies and personal factions allow voters to control the composition of the government but disdain or distort popular involvement. Governing caucuses, cause advocates, and office-seeking teams pursue their diverse visions of the public good, satisfying some interests but also neglecting civic development.

Ideological communities and social movements, in contrast, do involve their members in politics but are subject to rapid decay or manipulative domination. Urban machines enlist the emotional loyalties of their members in a larger cause but usually at the cost of loss of control over either leaders or policies. No perfect party exists, either in reality or even as a prescriptive model.

POLITICAL PARTIES AND DEMOCRATIC THEORY

These party concepts are ultimately tied to the most general arguments in democratic theory. In that long tradition, theorists often divide into two camps. On one side are the partisans of liberal democratic theory; emphasizing the human tendency to pursue self-interest, they suspect the uses of power and stress the consequent need to protect individuals against threats from other persons and from government. The other camp is the locus of communitarian democratic theory. More hopeful that humanity will respond favorably to moral training, these writers are more concerned with individual development. For these purposes they look more approvingly both on governmental programs and on extensive public participation to promote personal growth. Mansbridge insightfully describes these two traditions as "adversary democracy" and "unitary democracy."[28] Mill bridges the two groups, seeking both to limit power and to promote human development.

The first tradition is found in Hobbes, Locke, and, particularly in the United States, in Madison. Because of humans' self-interest, government is both necessary (particularly to Hobbes) and worrisome (especially to Locke). Madison summarizes the problem: "If men were angels, no government would be necessary. If angels were to govern men, neither external nor internal controls on government would be necessary." His solution is to use self-interest to promote the public good. "Ambition must be made to counteract ambition. The interest of the man must be connected with the constitutional rights of the place."[29]

The American liberal tradition stresses the democratic value of the exercise of control; achieving the other values depends on limitations of the political process. Interest optimization will be served better if government is not subject to intense popular demands, and personal development will flourish better if government is restrained.

The communitarian tradition derives from the ancient Greeks and from Rousseau and is best expressed in America by the Anti-Federalists. The principal democratic value is civic orientation. The exercise of control is seen by these theorists as only an enfeebled form of popular rule. Optimizing interests is expected to result from extensive participation, but participation itself is the most important goal.

These traditions are also evident in party concepts. Madison, in the tenth *Federalist*, is exemplary of the liberal tradition, with its emphasis on autonomous leadership and limited popular participation. Wise government consists of the management of factions, whose origins are "sown in the nature of man." That control requires a delegation of power to a "chosen body of citizens, whose wisdom may best discern the true interest of their country" and a limitation on the power of the electorate, prone "to sacrifice the weaker party or an obnoxious individual."[30]

Madison's own emphasis is on the ambiguous collective goal of the public good, paralleling the concept of party as a governing caucus. His theory, however, can easily accommodate other party models involving coalitional goals, such as the party as bureaucracy or the more accessible leadership of the party as office-seeking team.

The communitarian tradition is also evident in the party concepts, stressing collective goals, accessible leadership, and extensive participation. Although Rousseau clearly opposed political parties, he effectively advances these ideals, presenting a philosophy of politics similar to the model of party as a social movement. In Rousseau's view, politics should seek the collective general will, not particular interests, so that "when in the popular assembly a law is proposed, what the people is asked is not exactly whether it approves or rejects the proposal, but whether it is in conformity with the general will, which is their will." Leaders are accessible, with no authority other than to execute the policy decisions of the sovereign community. Civic development and full participation are the essence of good government, for "as soon as public service ceases to be the chief business of the citizens and they would rather serve with their money than with their persons, the State is not far from its fall."[31]

American parties have combined elements of both theoretical traditions, liberal and communitarian. They are composites, but not because of great theoretical commitments; they are the results more of experience than of reason. Typically originating in opposition to government, they share the liberal distrust of power. Arousing mass support, they reflect the communitarian faith in the "plain people." Seeking spoils and profit, they embody liberal individualism. Capturing the power of government, they implement visions of community welfare.

These parties have promoted each of the three democratic values yet have failed to achieve them fully. Their greatest success has been in actualizing the exercise of control over leadership, bringing peaceful and regular changes in the government. They have contributed, along with other institutions, to the satisfaction of policy interests, fostering considerable correspondence between popular preferences and public policy.[32]

This activity has been particularly evident when parties acted as governing caucuses (e.g., Wilson's New Freedom), as cohesive office-seeking teams (Roosevelt's New Deal), or as social movements (the antislavery Republican party). They have brought friendship as well as interests into politics, through urban machines and even personal factions, providing a necessary though incomplete emotional basis for the development of civic orientation.

The achievements of the American parties, however assessed, have been neither complete nor costless. Effective government requires power and therefore limits egalitarian civic participation. Similarly, the exercise of control inherently requires that there be identifiable political specialists— a party—who can be held accountable by the controlling public. And these persons, like all specialists, must be rewarded and will use their specialists' techniques for their own purposes.

Political control thus requires the vulgarity of officeseekers and the messiness of political competition. "The psycho-technics of party management and party advertising, slogans and marching tunes, are not accessories," Schumpeter emphasizes, "they are the essence of politics," for "democracy is the rule of the politician."[33]

POLITICAL PARTIES AND THE AMERICAN DEMOCRATIC FUTURE

If political parties have contributed to American democracy over the past two hundred years, their future service is uncertain. Trends both in American society generally and in the parties specifically raise problems, now widely recognized, that can be overcome only by deliberate action.

Difficulties exist in furthering each of the three values of democracy. The most problematic is the development of civic consciousness, which is also the most demanding standard of democracy. Civic consciousness has been nurtured traditionally in small communities, in close groups such as the family, and in interpersonal associations such as neighborhoods and unions. Face-to-face political associations, to Tocqueville, provided "large free schools, where all the members of the community go to learn the general theory of association" and the personal habits and techniques of democratic self-government.[34]

America continues to have a rich variety of voluntary associations, yet decline in this private order underlying public life has also been evident. It is marked by family instability, the spread of crime threatening neighborhood peace, extensive geographical mobility, the atrophy of unions, the replacement of community celebrations by mass-media entertainment, the incapacity of local government, and the bureaucratization of interest groups.

Political parties also evidence these weakened interpersonal ties. They are reflected in diminished party loyalties, the lessened impact of partisanship on voting behavior, and the replacement of the affective ties of local parties by the rational efficiency of national party bureaucracies.

Furthermore, optimizing group interests through democratic processes has become more difficult. American government still functions, to be sure, and has been reasonably successful in meeting some problems, such as economic growth and maintenance of American international power. Increasingly, however, dealing with problems is disjoined from popular decision on policy issues.

Many of the vital issues are now matters on which popular experience is inherently limited. For example, mass electorates do have some personal grasp of economic policy because they encounter inflation directly in the check-out lanes or experience unemployment. In contrast, newly dominant issues such as ecological balance or disarmament are technical, long-range, and unconnected to the voters' immediate, daily life. The result is that such problems must be handled by technical experts not subject to electoral control. Bureaucratic government may still be good government, but it is not democratic government.

This problem is worsened by political trends. The decline of local parties means that citizens know fewer political intermediaries who can explain these new problems or whom they can trust to reflect their experiences as decisions are made. Furthermore, close party competition at the national level induces timidity in policy innovation, and the continued partisan division between Congress and the president makes it virtually impossible for voters to assign clear responsibility for policy outcomes. Basic decisions, such as the federal budget deficit, are resolved in bipartisan negotiations, a "collusion of elites," in which politicians reach a plausible compromise but are then mutually safeguarded from open debate.[35]

The result is a weakening of the least difficult democratic value, the exercise of control. Policy control is particularly limited when voters cannot hold an indentifiable group accountable for either successes or errors in governmental programs. Yet voters still retain the ability to replace those in government with their electoral opponents, a powerful sanction to hold over individuals, such as a president.

American government, however, is not government by individuals; even presidential government is truly more than the actions of the single chief executive. Over the entire government and particularly over Congress, replacement of individuals has no cumulative effect. It is, as Woodrow Wilson warned, replacing only one cook instead of changing the recipe of the policy broth. In regard to this lack of clear responsibility, Hamilton's criticism of a diffuse government becomes newly relevant: "It often becomes impossible, amidst mutual accusations, to determine on whom the blame or the punishment of a pernicious measure, or a series of pernicious measures, ought really to fall."[36]

The problem is magnified by political trends that make candidates independent of the parties. Voters can occasionally remove a particular representative, but the advantages of office make most incumbents largely invulnerable if they avoid the most obvious corrupting temptations. Even a general mood of discontent against all incumbents, though evident in recent years, has no clear impact on policy.

At the same time, weakened party loyalties among the electorate make legislators more reliant on their own resources and potentially vulnerable to attack. To safeguard their isolated power, they are likely to take the safest course, devotedly follow public opinion, build personal factions, and limit their vision to the next election. Leadership toward the solution of national problems carries dangers but earns few rewards.

Countering these trends, other developments in American society and politics could lead to fuller realization of the basic democratic values. The American public itself has more resources for understanding politics, with an increased level of education. Simple self-interest has made politics more important to the population, as the number of people employed by government has increased and the potential personal benefit or harm of national governmental action has involved most people, from old-age pensioners to military reservists unexpectedly called to war duty to victims of unclean air and water.

With the dominance of the mass media and the evolution of centralized interest groups, American politics has become truly national. Even the weakened parties have responded to these trends, with increased ideological coherence among their legislators, activists, and mass base and with the development of effective national electioneering organizations.

THE FUTURE OF THE AMERICAN PARTY

The emergent national politics requires more effective national parties, a need now widely recognized. One commentator speaks for many in deploring the present state of American politics:

> Governing is turned into a perpetual campaign. Moreover, it makes government into an instrument designed to sustain an elected offi-

cial's public popularity. . . . The citizenry is viewed as a mass of fluid voters who can be appeased by appearances, occasional drama, and clever rhetoric. . . . The permanent campaign enshrines the pragmatism of the political party without the party. It appropriates the ideology of the American party—to the victor belong the spoils—without any constituency beyond phantom public opinion.[37]

Party reconstruction is the necessary alternative to this uncertain method of governance. National leadership, to be democratic, requires not only good presidents but widespread leadership, organized through the parties. As Huntington argues, "It is through such a system rather than broad appeals to public opinion that Presidents achieve the policy results they desire. Vigorous and responsible national leadership requires a network of petty tyrants."[38]

Reconstruction of the parties must be directed toward fuller realization of each of the democratic values, interest optimization, the exercise of control, and civic development. In the American context, no one party model can be fully applicable. Present trends, however, are bringing the parties too close to some models, such as cause advocates, office-seeking teams, bureaucracies, and personal factions. The nation would benefit if the parties developed more of the characteristics of ideological communities, social movements, governing caucuses, and even urban machines.

The purpose of change is not to make American parties fit any one model but to move the system incrementally along the three dimensions toward fuller participation, a greater concern for collective goals, and more autonomous leadership. The following proposed changes, none requiring Constitutional amendment, would move American parties in these directions.[39] This program recognizes the trends in voter behavior and the problems inherent in the reforms analyzed in chapters 7 and 8. American parties will remain groups that seek power through elections under their common label. We cannot expect them to become models of intellectual debate or of participatory democracy; however, we can envisage the parties as leadership coalitions with a heightened degree of policy coherence, supported by a more active mass base. These suggested changes are unusual but not impossible to imagine or to achieve. Every one of these proposals, in fact, is established practice either in some state in the American Union or in other liberal democracies. So, let us begin.

—Nominations for public office should be made only by party members, either in closed primaries or, better, by mail ballot among persons who have personally enrolled in the party and paid modest dues. The dues could be collected through the income-tax checkoff to avoid any discriminatory effect on low-income voters. This procedure would make the parties' prospective leaders responsible to a broad popular base, promote coherence in the policy perspective of the parties, and provide members with significant impact on the choice of candidates. These qualities could also be advanced by nominating candidates in party caucuses and conventions, but Americans' distrust of parties probably makes it impossible to recreate these past practices.

—Preceding membership decisions on nominations, party conventions should recommend candidates for statewide or federal office, including the president. These conventions should include a large proportion of party leaders and public officials elected under the party label, perhaps half of the total. At the national conventions, illustratively, the delegates would include all governors, congressmen, and U.S. senators as well as delegates elected from local party branches. Candidates receiving a prescribed minimum vote at the conventions (perhaps 20 percent) would then be presented to the party members for their decision, through televised debates and mailed leaflets. This combination would induce greater coherence in government among party candidates and give rank-and-file members a vital role within the party, stimulating their civic consciousness.

These conventions also should debate and adopt the party platform, developed over the preceding year by party policy commissions, which would include a substantial number of party officeholders and the holding of national hearings. In place of the rushed deliberations at conventions, these commissions would promote more thorough consideration and foster the development of consensual party programs. This mechanism would aid both citizen control of policy and citizen development and avoid unrealistic attempts to impose party discipline on public officials. The procedure would also probably contribute to more unified party action within government, further simplifying popular control. Institutional change within the congressional parties would further enhance control, through such devices as more active party caucuses or the adoption of a formal "shadow cabinet" by the minority party.

—Party resources, especially money, should be expanded through legislation, fostering contributions to parties but not to candidates. Appropriate techniques might include matching income-tax checkoffs, reviving the income-tax deduction for party contributions, and eliminating the limits on party contributions to candidates but retaining limits on individual and group contributions. Following the precedent of the government's paying for the national conventions, the federal treasury should provide a fixed, unconditional subsidy for the interelection costs of administering the national parties.

Legislation could also reduce the need for party fund-raising, for example, by providing the parties either free or government-paid uncensored time on television for party political broadcasts, mailing party brochures to all voters, and mandating the lowest commercial charges for party broadcasts and mail. These public funds should be contingent on the parties' agreement to sponsor and hold televised debates among presidential, vice-presidential, and statewide candidates.

Increased party financing can be used to revitalize the parties' local grass roots. As an incentive, funds collected within the party candidates' own state could be matched in higher ratios than those from other areas of the nation. Regulation of finances could also restrict the proportion of public funds that could be spent on mass-media advertising, thereby encouraging more interpersonal campaigning.

—Voter registration should become a responsibility of government, using governmental agencies such as motor vehicle departments to enroll residents and the postal service to register voters who change residence. Registering to vote should carry with it the opportunity to enroll in a party and to pay its dues. By broadening the potential electorate, greater opportunities will exist for full civic participation, including partisan activity. By relieving parties of the burden of registration, they will be better able to deal with issues of public policy.

—State legislation should be amended or challenged in the courts to reduce the severe restraints on parties. The parties should be generally left free to determine their own internal organization and membership qualifications, to decide on their campaign activities, to handle their own funds and staffs, and to recommend patronage appointments. Legislation is needed only to prevent financial fraud and racial or sexual discrimination in primaries and in similar governmental activities. By freeing the parties, their leaders will gain more responsibility and their members achieve more control and greater civic consciousness.

—The parties can take further action toward their own renewal, particularly when they are provided with new financial resources. They might consider such local activities as ombudsmen services, issue forums, and sponsorship of civic programs. At the national level, they might operate a cable television network, distribute their message through third-class mass mailings, and offer selective incentives such as cooperative purchasing to potential members. Through such techniques, the parties would become more effective agencies, facilitating popular control.

As the parties gained resources and members, they would become more significant campaign participants. This renewal would provide incentives for candidates to build a party, not an individual, record. With greater institutional capacity, the parties would be more likely to develop coherent policy programs. With more support from the parties, candidates could be more secure in considering long-range national problems. By stimulating individual financial contributions to parties, these measures would also encourage individual local participation, increasing civic consciousness.

This program will not solve all the problems of American political parties, much less those of American government generally. Human incapacity and self-centeredness will continue. Madison's judgment still applies: Men and women are not angels who can live without government, and politicians are not angels who can govern without constraint.

These measures may make a start, however. Their adoption may begin to redirect the undoubted ambitions of American politicians toward greater concern for collective goals, begin to allow politicians to use more of their considerable intellectual and personal skills toward meeting national problems, and begin to encourage a more robust civic consciousness among the electorate.

Democracy, like life itself, is a process, never a complete achievement. Michels appropriately provides our final lesson. He repeats an old tale of a dying farmer who told his children of a treasure buried in the fields of the family farm. After extended plowing, they found no buried gold, but their hard work resulted in a magnificent harvest. Michels's moral might be our own: "Democracy is a treasure which no one will ever discover by deliberate search. But in continuing our search, in laboring indefatigably to discover the undiscoverable, we shall perform a work which will have fertile results."[40]

NOTES

PREFACE

1. Alan Ware, *Citizens, Parties, and the State* (Princeton, N.J.; Princeton University Press, 1987), p. 1.

CHAPTER ONE: CONCEPTS OF POLITICAL PARTIES

1. *New York Times*, January 3, 1990.

2. The commitment came in the forty-two signatures to the agreement establishing the European Bank: Ibrahim Shibata, *The European Bank for Reconstruction and Development* (London: Graham and Trottman, 1990), p. 109. Marc Pomper kindly provided this reference.

3. E. E. Schattschneider, *Party Government* (New York: Holt, Rinehart and Winston, 1942), p. 1.

4. More recent major works include Ian Budge, Ivor Crewe, and Dennis Fairlie, eds., *Party Identification and Beyond* (London: Wiley, 1976); Hans Daadler and Peter Mair, eds., *Western European Party Systems* (Beverly Hills, Calif.: Sage Publications, 1983); Kenneth Janda, *Political Parties: A Cross-National Survey* (New York: Free Press, 1980); Kay Lawson, *The Comparative Study of Political Parties* (New York: St. Martin's Press, 1975); Seymour Lipset and Stein Rokkan, *Party Systems and Voter Alignments* (New York: Free Press, 1967); Peter Merkl, *Western European Party Systems* (New York: Free Press, 1980); and Giovanni Sartori, *Parties and Party Systems* (Cambridge: Cambridge University Press, 1976).

5. *Thoughts on the Cause of the Present Discontents* (1770), in Paul Langford, ed., *The Writings and Speeches of Edmund Burke* (Oxford: Clarendon Press, 1981), p. 317.

6. Sartori, *Parties*, p. 26; italics in the original.

7. James Madison, *The Federalist*, No. 10 (1787; New York: Modern Library, 1941), p. 54.

8. Albert Hirschman, *The Passions and the Interests* (Princeton, N.J.: Princeton University Press, 1977).

9. Leon Epstein, *Political Parties in Western Democracies* (New Brunswick, N.J.: Transaction Publishers, 1979), p. 9.

10. Sartori, *Parties*, p. 64; italics in the original omitted.

11. Kay Lawson, ed., *Political Parties and Linkage* (New Haven, Conn.: Yale University Press, 1980), p. 3.

12. These specific phrases are from Frank Sorauf and Paul Beck, *Party Politics in America*, 6th ed. (Glenview, Ill.: Scott, Foresman, 1988). The basic framework was

established in the five editions of V. O. Key, *Politics, Parties, and Pressure Groups*, 5th ed. (New York: Crowell, 1964).

13. Denise L. Baer and David A. Bositis, *Elite Cadres and Party Coalitions* (Westport, Conn.: Greenwood Press, 1988), pp. 13, 23.

14. Joseph Schlesinger, "On the Theory of Party Organization," *Journal of Politics* 46 (May 1984): 377.

15. Schattschneider, *Party Government*, p. 59.

16. These dimensions have a family resemblance to those developed by Joseph Schlesinger to define parties: market orientation, collective goals, and indirect incentives. In the approach used here, these characteristics are regarded not as constant features of any political party but as themselves varying among party concepts. See Schlesinger, "Theory," 369–400.

17. The figures in this chapter were machine-drawn by Patricia Michaels and Rayna Pomper and are gratefully acknowledged here.

18. A notable example is John Kessel, *Presidential Campaign Politics*, 4th ed. (Pacific Grove, Calif.: Brooks/Cole, 1992).

19. Woodrow Wilson, in *Inaugural Addresses of the Presidents of the United States* (Washington, D.C.: Government Printing Office, 1989), pp. 227–29.

20. W. L. Riordan, *Plunkitt of Tammany Hall* (New York: Dutton, 1963), p. 88.

21. Austin Ranney makes a similar distinction between competitive and expressive parties: *Curing the Mischiefs of Faction* (Berkeley: University of California Press, 1975), pp. 134–42.

22. See, for example, Larry Sabato, *The Rise of Political Consultants* (New York: Basic Books, 1981), and Barbara Salmore and Stephen Salmore, *Candidates, Parties, and Campaigns*, 2d ed. (Washington, D.C.: Congressional Quarterly Press, 1989).

23. Anthony Downs, *An Economic Theory of Democracy* (New York: Harper, 1957), pp. 27–28.

24. Maurice Duverger, *Political Parties* (London: Methuen, 1954), p. 125, drawing on Frederick Tonnies's concept of "gemeinschaft."

25. James Q. Wilson, *Political Organizations* (New York: Basic Books, 1973), chap. 6.

26. V. I. Lenin, *What Is to Be Done?* (New York: International Publishers, 1929), p. 116.

27. Robert Michels, *Political Parties*, ed. Seymour Martin Lipset (1915; New York: Collier Books, 1962).

28. Committee on Political Parties, "Toward a More Responsible Two-Party System," *American Political Science Review* 44 (Sept. 1950): *Supplement*.

29. M. Ostrogorski, *Democracy and the Organization of Political Parties*, ed. Seymour Martin Lipset, 2 vols. (1902; New York: Doubleday Anchor, 1964), esp. vol. 2.

30. William Kornhauser, *The Politics of Mass Society* (New York: Free Press, 1959).

31. Joseph Schumpeter, *Capitalism, Socialism, and Democracy* (New York: Harper, 1950), p. 269.

32. See Hanna Pitkin's discussion in *The Concept of Representation* (Berkeley: University of California Press, 1967), chaps. 6–8.

33. See the work of Arend Lijphart, beginning with *The Politics of Accommodation* (Berkeley: University of California Press, 1968).

CHAPTER TWO: INTERESTS WITHOUT PASSIONS

1. Martin Van Buren, *Autobiography*, in *Annual Report of the American Historical Association, 1918*, 2 vols. (1854; Washington, D. C.: Government Printing Office, 1920), 2: 519n. Carolyn Nestor kindly provided me with this quotation and with much of this chapter's research material on Van Buren.

2. Robert Michels, *Political Parties*, ed. Seymour Martin Lipset (1915; New York: Collier Books, 1962), p. 365.

3. The full story is well told by Robert Remini, *Martin Van Buren and the Making of the Democratic Party* (New York: Columbia University Press, 1959).

4. Richard Hofstadter, *The Idea of a Party System* (Berkeley: University of California Press, 1970), p. 246.

5. Michels, *Political Parties*, p. 336.

6. Ibid., pp. 78–79.

7. A. C. McLaughlin, *The Courts, the Constitution and Parties* (Chicago: University of Chicago Press, 1912), p. 112.

8. Richard Jensen, "Party Coalitions and the Search for Modern Values: 1820–1970," in *Party Coalitions in the 1980s*, ed. Seymour Lipset (San Francisco: Institute for Contemporary Studies, 1981), p. 67.

9. Silas Wright, quoted in Hofstadter, *Idea of a Party System*, p. 244.

10. Alvin Kass, *Politics in New York State, 1800–1830* (Syracuse, N. Y.: Syracuse University Press, 1965), p. 29.

11. Quoted in Hofstadter, *Idea of a Party System*, p. 250.

12. Michels, *Political Parties*, pp. 170, 182.

13. *Branti* v. *Finkel*, 445 U.S. 590 (1980).

14. Remini, *Making of the Democratic Party*, p. 126.

15. Donald B. Cole, *Martin Van Buren and the American Political System* (Princeton, N. J.: Princeton University Press, 1984), p. 267.

16. Amitai Etzioni, "Two Approaches to Organizational Effectiveness," *American Sociological Quarterly* 5 (Sept. 1960): 257–78.

17. Michels, *Political Parties*, p. 364.

18. Michael Wallace, "Changing Concepts of Party in the United States: New York, 1815–1828," *American Historical Review* 74 (1969): p. 460.

19. Richard P. McCormick, *The Second American Party System* (Chapel Hill: University of North Carolina Press, 1966), esp. chap. 7.

20. Hofstadter, *Idea of a Party System*, p. 225.

21. Cornelius Cotter, James Gibson, John Bibby, and Robert Huckshorn, *Party Organizations in American Politics* (New York: Praeger, 1984), p. 155. A later article finds a continuation of these trends: James Gibson, John Frendreis, and Laura Vertz, "Party Dynamics in the 1980s," *American Journal of Political Science*, 33 (Feb. 1989): 67–90.

22. Cotter et al., *Party Organizations*, pp. 32–33.

23. Ibid., pp. 16, 18, and 36 n. 1. The authors claim that the consumer price index's (CPI's) increasing 275 percent is not a valid measure of the effect of inflation on party budgets (which increased less than 100 percent). Major items in the CPI, however, such as housing, food, and benefits, would probably be reflected in party budgets for headquarters or staff. Moreover, parties faced unusual inflationary pressures in this period in above-average increases for transportation, postage, and media.

24. Paul Herrnson, *Party Campaigning in the 1980s* (Cambridge, Mass.: Harvard University Press, 1988), p. 46.

25. Federal Election Commission, "FEC Releases Summary of 1989–90 Political Party Finances" (March 15, 1991); *National Journal* 22 (June 16, 1990); 1472.

26. Leon Epstein, *Political Parties in the American Mold* (Madison: University of Wisconsin Press, 1986), p. 238 and chap. 7. Herrnson, *Party Campaigning*, is the best description of these national parties.

27. Michels, *Political Parties*, p. 108.

28. Robert Huckshorn, *Party Leadership in the States* (Amherst: University of Massachusetts Press, 1976).

29. Barbara Salmore and Stephen Salmore, *Candidates, Parties and Campaigns*, 2d ed. (Washington, D. C.: Congressional Quarterly Press, 1989), p. 255.

30. Federal Election Commission, *Congressional Quarterly Weekly Report* 48 (Dec. 23, 1990): 4235.

31. Michael Johnston, "Patrons and Clients, Jobs and Machines," *American Political Science Review* 73 (June, 1979): 385–98; Frank Sorauf, *Party and Representation* (New York: Atherton, 1963); Gerald Pomper, Rodney Forth, and Maureen Moakley, "Another Machine Withers Away," in *American Politics and Public Policy*, ed. Allan Sindler (Washington, D. C.: Congressional Quarterly Press, 1982), chap. 5.

32. The differences in these organizations are developed brilliantly by Joseph Schlesinger, "On the Theory of Party Competition," *Journal of Politics* 46 (May 1984): 369–400.

33. See Gerald Pomper, "Party Organization and Electoral Success," *Polity* 23 (Winter 1990): 190–91.

34. Michels, *Political Parties*, pp. 338–39.

35. See David Runkel, ed., *Campaign for President: The Managers Look at '88* (Westport, Conn.: Greenwood, 1989).

36. Max Weber, "Politics as a Vocation," in *From Max Weber*, ed. H. H. Gerth and C. Wright Mills (New York: Oxford University Press, 1958), p. 84; italics in the original omitted.

37. Michels, *Political Parties*, p. 207.

38. Ibid., p. 87.

39. Wilson Carey McWilliams, "Parties as Civic Associations," in *Party Renewal in America*, ed. Gerald Pomper (New York: Praeger, 1980), p. 63.

40. Michels, *Political Parties*, p. 61.

41. Denise Baer and David Bositis, *Elite Cadres and Party Coalitions* (New York: Greenwood Press, 1988).

42. G. Bingham Powell, Jr., "American Voter Turnout in Comparative Perspective," *American Political Science Review* 80 (March 1986); 17–44. On the effect of parties within the United States today, see Gregory Caldeira, Samuel Patterson, and Gregory Markko, "The Mobilization of Voters in Congressional Elections,"*Journal of Politics* 47 (May 1985); 490–505. The historical decline is analyzed by Walter Dean Burnham, *Critical Elections* (New York: Norton, 1970), esp. chap. 4, and Paul Kleppner, *Who Voted?* (New York: Praeger, 1982).

43. M. Ostrogorski, *Democracy and the Organization of Political Parties*, ed. Seymour Martin Lipset, 2 vols. (1902; New York: Doubleday Anchor, 1964), Vol. 2: p. 35.

44. Hofstadter, *Idea of a Party System*, p. 242.

45. George Washington, "Farewell Address," in *Messages and Papers of the*

Presidents, ed. James Richardson (Washington, D.C.: Government Printing Office, 1897), p. 209.

46. Van Buren, *Autobiography*, p. 125.

47. Michels, *Political Parties*, p. 371.

CHAPTER THREE: COMMON INTERESTS

1. Woodrow Wilson, in *Inaugural Addresses of the Presidents of the United States* (Washington, D.C.: Government Printing Office, 1989), p. 228.

2. Wendell Willkie, "The Function of a Political Party," *Vital Speeches of the Day* 10 (April 1, 1944): 359–60.

3. Ronald Reagan, accepting the Republican nomination, in *Vital Speeches of the Day* 50 (Sept. 15, 1984): 706.

4. Wilson, in *Inaugural Addresses*, p. 229.

5. Woodrow Wilson, "A Nonpartisan Talk to the Commercial Club of Omaha, Nebraska," in *The Papers of Woodrow Wilson*, ed. Arthur S. Link (1912; Princeton, N.J.: Princeton University Press, 1978), 25: 346.

6. Woodrow Wilson, *Congressional Government* (1885; Boston: Houghton Mifflin, 1925), p. 332.

7. Austin Ranney, *The Doctrine of Responsible Party Government* (Urbana: University of Illinois Press, 1954), p. 30.

8. Woodrow Wilson, "Committee or Cabinet Government?" (1884), in *Papers of Woodrow Wilson* (1967), 2:624.

9. Ibid., pp. 623–27.

10. Woodrow Wilson, *Constitutional Government in the United States* (1908; New York: Columbia University Press, 1961), pp. 67–68.

11. See Jeffrey Tulis, *The Rhetorical Presidency* (Princeton, N. J.: Princeton University Press, 1987).

12. Committee on Political Parties, "Toward a More Responsible Two-Party System," *American Political Science Review* 44 (Sept. 1950): *Supplement*, 1.

13. Joseph Schlesinger, "The Primary Goals of Political Parties," *American Political Science Review* 69 (Sept. 1975): 840–49.

14. David Mayhew, *Congress: The Electoral Connection* (New Haven, Conn.: Yale University Press, 1974), p. 99.

15. John Kingdon notes the "congratulation-rationalization effect" on legislative candidates, in *Candidates for Office* (New York: Random House, 1968).

16. Samuel Kernell, "Explaining Presidential Popularity," *American Political Science Review* 72 (June 1978): 506–22; Douglas Rivers and Nancy Rose, "Passing the President's Program," *American Journal of Political Science* 29 (May 1985): 183–96.

17. Jack Walker, "Setting the Agenda in the U.S. Senate," *British Journal of Political Science* 7 (Oct. 1977): 423–45; Nelson Polsby, *Political Innovation in America* (New Haven, Conn.: Yale University Press, 1984).

18. Cornelius Cotter, James Gibson, John Bibby, and Robert Huckshorn, *Party Organizations in American Politics* (New York: Praeger, 1984), pp. 90–91.

19. Anthony Downs, *An Economic Theory of Democracy* (New York: Harper, 1957), chap. 4.

20. Morris Fiorina, *Retrospective Voting in American National Elections* (New Haven, Conn.: Yale University Press, 1981), p. 78.

21. *The Gallup Poll: Public Opinion 1988* (Wilmington, Del.: Scholarly Resources, 1989), Sept. 9–11, p. 166.

22. Stanley Kelley, Jr., *Interpreting Elections* (Princeton, N. J.: Princeton University Press, 1983).

23. Richard F. Fenno, Jr., *Home Style* (Boston: Little Brown, 1978), p. 168.

24. *Congressional Quarterly Weekly Report* 48 (Dec. 22, 1990): 4188–91. See David Rohde, *Parties and Leaders in the Postreform House* (Chicago: University of Chicago Press, 1991).

25. John Sullivan and Robert O'Connor, "Electoral Choice and Popular Control of Public Policy," *American Political Science Review* 66 (Dec. 1972): 1256–68.

26. Richard Rose, *Do Parties Make a Difference?* (Chatham, N.J.: Chatham House, 1980), chap. 8.

27. Richard Dawson and James Robinson, "Interparty Competition, Economic Variables, and Welfare Policies in the American States," *Journal of Politics* 24 (May 1963): 265–89; Thomas Dye, *Politics, Economics, and the Public* (Chicago: Rand McNally, 1966).

28. Alan Monroe, "American Party Platforms and Public Opinion," *American Journal of Political Science* 27 (Feb. 1983): 27–42.

29. Gerald Pomper, with Susan Lederman, *Elections in America*, 2d ed. (New York: Longman, 1980), pp. 162–69.

30. Brian Fry and Richard Winters, "The Politics of Redistribution," *American Political Science Review* 64 (June 1970): 508–22; Edward Jennings, "Competition, Constituencies and Welfare Policies in the American States," *American Political Science Review* 73 (June 1979): 414–29; Charles Cnudde and Donald McCrone, "Party Competition and Welfare Policies in the American States," *American Political Science Review* 63 (Sept. 1969): 858–66.

31. Robert Erikson, Gerald Wright, Jr., and John McIver, "Political Parties, Public Opinion, and State Policy in the United States," *American Political Science Review* 83 (Sept. 1989): 729–50.

32. Douglas Hibbs, "Political Parties and Macroeconomic Policy," *American Political Science Review* 71 (Dec. 1977): 1467–87.

33. Ian Budge and Richard Hofferbert, "Mandates and Policy Outputs: U.S. Party Platforms and Federal Expenditures," *American Political Science Review* 84 (March 1990): 111–31.

34. James Madison, *The Federalist*, No. 10 (1787; New York: Modern Library, 1941), p. 62.

35. Arthur S. Link, *Woodrow Wilson: Revolution, War, and Peace* (Arlington Heights, Ill.: AHM Publishing, 1979), p. 125.

36. Benjamin Ginsberg and Martin Shefter, *Politics by Other Means* (New York: Basic Books, 1990), p. 32 and chaps. 1, 6.

37. M. Ostrogorski, *Democracy and the Organization of Political Parties*, ed. Seymour Martin Lipset, 2 vols. (1902; New York: Doubleday Anchor, 1964), 2: 356.

38. John Kessel, *Presidential Campaign Politics* (Homewood, Ill.: Dorsey, 1980), 66; John Kessel, John Bruce, and John Clark, "Advocacy Politics in Presidential Parties," *American Political Science Review* 85 (Dec. 1991): 1089–1106.

39. V. O. Key, *Politics, Parties, and Pressure Groups*, 5th ed. (New York: Crowell, 1964), p. 280.

40. Peter Odegard, *Pressure Politics: The Story of the Anti-Saloon League* (New York: Columbia University Press, 1928).

41. Edmund Burke, "Speech to the Electors of Bristol," in *Works* (1774; Boston: Little Brown, 1866), 2: 89–98.

42. Ranney, *Doctrine*, p. 39.

43. Wilson, *Constitutional Government*, pp. 221–22.

44. Ibid., p. 222.

45. Warren Miller and Kent Jennings, *Parties in Transition* (New York: Russell Sage, 1986), chap. 9; Warren Miller, *Without Consent* (Lexington: University Press of Kentucky, 1988), chap. 3.

46. Martin Plissner and Warren Mitofsky, "The Making of the Delegates, 1968–1988," *Public Opinion* 11 (Sept./Oct. 1988): 46.

47. Walter Bate, "Introduction," in *Selected Writings of Edmund Burke* (New York: Modern Library, 1960), p. 34. I am indebted to Joseph Romance for this reference.

48. Max Weber, "Politics as a Vocation," in *From Max Weber*, ed. H. H. Gerth and C. Wright Mills (New York: Oxford University Press, 1958), p. 128.

CHAPTER FOUR: COMMON PASSIONS

1. V. I. Lenin, *What Is to Be Done?* (New York: International Publishers, 1929), pp. 32f.

2. V. I. Lenin, "One Step Forward, Two Steps Backward," in *On Organization* (New York: Workers' Library, 1926), p. 127.

3. Lenin, *What Is to Be Done?* p. 28.

4. Ibid., p. 15.

5. Ibid., pp. 14, 28

6. V. I. Lenin, *"Left-Wing" Communism: An Infantile Disorder* (New York: International Publishers, 1934), p. 28.

7. Lenin, "One Step Forward," p. 174.

8. V. I. Lenin, "A Letter to a Comrade on Our Problems of Organization," in *On Organization*, p. 112.

9. V. I. Lenin, "The Reorganization of the Party," *Selected Works* (New York: International Publishers, 1952), 3: 456.

10. Lenin, *What Is to Be Done?* p. 42.

11. Lenin, *"Left-Wing" Communism*, p. 78.

12. V. I. Lenin, *State and Revolution* (New York: International Publishers, 1932), p. 34.

13. Lawrence Goodwyn, *The Populist Moment* (New York: Oxford University Press, 1978), pp. 33–35.

14. "People's Platform of 1892," in *National Party Platforms*, ed. Donald B. Johnson, 2 vols. (Urbana: University of Illinois Press, 1978), 1: 89–91.

15. Lawrence Goodwyn, *Democratic Promise* (New York: Oxford University Press, 1976), p. xv.

16. Goodwyn, *Populist Moment*, p. 56.

17. Ibid., pp. 231–32.

18. Amos Pinchot, *History of the Progressive Party*, ed. Helene Maxwell Hooker (New York: NYU Press, 1958), pp. 171–72.

19. S. J. Duncan-Clark, *The Progressive Movement* (Boston: Small, Maynard, 1913), p. 42.

20. Richard Hofstadter, *The Progressive Movement* (Englewood Cliffs, N.J.: Prentice-Hall, 1963), p. 5.

21. Arthur S. Link and Richard L. McCormick, *Progressivism* (Arlington Heights, Ill.: Harlan Davidson, 1983), pp. 23–24.

22. Milovan Djilas, *The New Class* (New York: Praeger, 1957), pp. 39, 47.

23. See Mancur Olson, *The Logic of Collective Action* (Cambridge, Mass.: Harvard University Press, 1965).

24. Clinton Rossiter, *Parties and Politics in America* (Ithaca, N.Y.: Cornell University Press, 1960), pp. 11, 59.

25. Peggy Noonan, *What I Saw at the Revolution* (New York: Random House, 1990), p. 15. A more academic but equally pointed critique was made by Jeane Kirkpatrick in *The New Presidential Elite* (New York: Russell Sage, 1976).

26. Nelson Polsby and Aaron Wildavsky, *Presidential Elections*, 7th ed. (New York: Free Press, 1988), pp. 27–28.

27. James Q. Wilson, *The Amateur Democrat* (Chicago: University of Chicago Press, 1962), p. 127.

28. Herbert McClosky, Paul J. Hoffman, and Rosemary O'Hara, "Issue Conflict and Consensus among Party Leaders and Followers," *American Political Science Review* 54 (June 1960): 406–27.

29. Ronald Rapoport, Alan Abramowitz, and John McGlennon, *The Life of the Parties* (Lexington: University Press of Kentucky, 1986), chap. 3, p. 50.

30. Warren Miller and M. Kent Jennings, *Parties in Transition* (New York: Russell Sage, 1986); Warren Miller, *Without Consent* (Lexington: University Press of Kentucky, 1988).

31. Denise L. Baer and David A. Bositis, *Elite Cadres and Party Coalitions* (New York: Greenwood Press, 1988), p. 183.

32. Miller and Jennings, *Parties in Transition*, pp. 97, 84; the quotation is on p. 96.

33. Alan Abramowitz and Walter Stone, *Nomination Politics* (New York: Praeger, 1984), pp. 84, 110.

34. Kirkpatrick, *New Presidential Elite*. For a parallel in Great Britain, see David Kogan and Maurice Kogan, *The Battle for the Labour Party* (London: Kegan Paul, 1982).

35. John Aldrich, "A Downsian Spatial Model with Party Activism," *American Political Science Review* 77 (Dec. 1983): 974–90.

36. A. C. McLaughlin, *The Courts, the Constitution and Parties* (Chicago: University of Chicago Press, 1912), p. 134.

37. Robert Michels, *Political Parties*, ed. Seymour Martin Lipset (1915; New York: Collier Books, 1962), p. 271. Olson, *Logic of Collective Action*, provides the theoretical understanding of these developments.

38. Quoted in Bertram Wolfe, *Three Who Made a Revolution* (Boston: Beacon Press, 1955), p. 253.

39. John Stuart Mill, *On Liberty*, chap. 2, ll. 36–43 (1859; New York: Appleton-Century-Crofts, 1947), p. 16.

40. Alexis de Tocqueville, *Democracy in America*, ed. Phillips Bradley, 2 vols. (1835/1840; New York: Vintage, 1954), 1: 271.

41. David Barnum and John Sullivan, "The Elusive Foundations of Political Freedom in Britain and the United States," *Journal of Politics* 52 (Aug. 1990): 719–39;

John Sullivan, James Piereson, and George Marcus, *Political Tolerance and American Democracy* (Chicago: University of Chicago Press, 1982).

CHAPTER FIVE: PASSIONATE INTERESTS

1. William L. Riordan, *Plunkitt of Tammany Hall* (New York: E. P. Dutton, 1963), p. 13.

2. Seymour Mandlebaum, *Boss Tweed's New York* (New York: Wiley, 1965).

3. M. Ostrogorski, *Democracy and the Organization of Political Parties*, ed. Seymour Lipset, 2 vols. (1902; New York: Doubleday Anchor, 1964), 2: 209–11.

4. The classic analysis is Robert Merton, "The Latent Functions of the Political Machine," in *Social Theory and Social Structure*, rev. ed. (New York: Free Press, 1957), pp. 72–82.

5. Among the extensive and enjoyable literature on "bosses" are Walton Bean, *Boss Ruef's San Francisco* (Berkeley: University of California Press, 1952); Edward Flynn, *You're the Boss* (New York: Collier Books, 1962); Dayton McKean, *The Boss* (Boston: Houghton Mifflin, 1940); and John Salter, *Boss Rule: Portraits in City Politics* (London: McGraw-Hill, 1925).

6. Lincoln Steffens, *The Shame of the Cities* (1904; New York: Hill and Wang, 1957), pp. 11, 142–43.

7. Edward C. Banfield and James Q. Wilson, *City Politics* (Cambridge, Mass.: Harvard University Press and MIT Press, 1963), p. 115; italics in the original.

8. Ostrogorski, *Democracy*, p. 211.

9. Riordan, *Plunkitt*, p. 14.

10. Raymond Wolfinger, "Why Machines Have Not Withered Away and Other Revisionist Thoughts," *Journal of Politics* 34 (May 1972): 365–98.

11. Harold Gosnell, *Machine Politics: Chicago Model*, 2d ed. (1937; Chicago: University of Chicago Press, 1968), chaps. 2–4, and Sonya Forthal, *Cogwheels of Democracy* (1946; Westport, Conn.: Greenwood, 1972).

12. Steven P. Erie, *Rainbow's End* (Berkeley: University of California Press, 1988), p. 10.

13. Chester Barnard, *The Functions of the Executive* (Cambridge, Mass.: Harvard University Press, 1938); Amitai Etzioni, "Two Approaches to Organizational Effectiveness," *American Sociological Quarterly* 5 (Sept. 1960): 257–78.

14. Michael Johnston, "Patrons and Clients, Jobs and Machines," *American Political Science Review* 73 (June 1979): 385–98.

15. Kenneth Mladenka, "The Urban Bureaucracy and the Chicago Political Machine," *American Political Science Review* 74 (Dec. 1980): 991–98.

16. Frank Sorauf, *Party and Representation* (New York: Atherton, 1963).

17. Edward N. Costikyan, *Behind Closed Doors* (New York: Harcourt Brace, 1966), p. 334. Chapters 22 and 23 are excellent discussions of the limits and problems of patronage.

18. See Gerald Pomper, Rodney Forth, and Maureen Moakley, "Another Machine Withers Away: For Better? For Worse?" in *American Politics and Public Policy*, ed. Allan Sindler (Washington, D. C.: Congressional Quarterly Press, 1982), chap. 5.

19. Riordan, *Plunkitt*, pp. 82, 70.

20. Erie, *Rainbow's End*, particularly chaps. 3 and 4.

21. Lincoln Steffens, *The Autobiography of Lincoln Steffens* (New York: Harcourt Brace, 1931), p. 618.

22. Riordan, *Plunkitt*, p. 28.

23. Henry Jones Ford, *The Rise and Growth of American Politics* (New York: Macmillan, 1914), p. 307.

24. See John Allswang, *Bosses, Machines, and Urban Voters* (Baltimore: Johns Hopkins University Press, 1977); Martin Shefter, "The Electoral Foundations of the Political Machine: New York City, 1884–1897," in *The History of American Electoral Behavior*, ed. Joel Silbey, Allan Bogue, and William Flanigan (Princeton, N.J.: Princeton University Press, 1978), pp. 263–98.

25. See Nathan Glazer and Daniel Moynihan, *Beyond the Melting Pot* (1963; Cambridge, Mass.: MIT Press, 1970).

26. Thomas M. Guterbock, *Machine Politics in Transition: Party and Community in Chicago* (Chicago: University of Chicago Press, 1980), p. 280.

27. On LaGuardia, see Arthur Mann, *LaGuardia Comes to Power* (Philadelphia: Lippincott, 1965); on Brand Whitlock, see his autobiography, *Forty Years of It* (New York: Appleton, 1914). I am indebted to Cliff Fox for the latter reference.

28. Erie, *Rainbow's End*, pp. 211f.

29. For a classic description of ethnic turnover, see Robert Dahl, *Who Governs?* (New Haven, Conn.: Yale University Press, 1961), chap. 4.

30. William F. Whyte, *Street Corner Society*, 3d ed. (Chicago: University of Chicago Press, 1981), pp. 245–50.

31. Steffens, *Shame of the Cities*, p. 3.

32. Amy Bridges, *A City in the Republic: Antebellum New York and the Origins of Machine Politics* (New York: Cambridge University Press, 1984).

33. Gosnell, *Machine Politics*, pp. 70–73.

34. Bruce Stave, *The New Deal and the Last Hurrah: Pittsburgh Machine Politics* (University of Pittsburg Press, 1970)

35. Bridges, *City in the Republic*.

36. Thucydides, *The Peloponnesian War*, trans. Rex Warner (London: Penguin Books, 1954), pp. 147, 149.

CHAPTER SIX: INTERESTS AND PASSIONS

1. Jeremy Bentham, *An Introduction to the Principles of Morals and Legislation*, ed. Laurence LaFleur (1789; New York: Hafner, 1948), chap. 1, pp. 2, 187–88.

2. Anthony Downs, *An Economic Theory of Democracy* (New York: Harper & Row, 1957), p. 28.

3. Bentham, *Principles*, chap. 1, p. 1.

4. Ibid., chap. 4, pp. 29–32; Jeremy Bentham, *A Fragment on Government*, Preface, 2 (1776; Westport, Conn.: Greenwood, 1980), p. 93.

5. Downs, *Economic Theory*, pp. 36–40.

6. Ibid., pp. 53–55.

7. Ibid., p. 28.

8. A. C. McLaughlin, *The Courts, the Constitution and Parties* (Chicago: University of Chicago Press, 1912), pp. 133–35.

9. Downs, *Economic Theory*, p. 136. Martin Wattenberg further extends the appli-

cation of Downs's theory to recent presidential elections. See *The Rise of Candidate-Centered Politics* (Cambridge, Mass.: Harvard University Press, 1991), chap. 1.

10. Joseph Schlesinger, "On the Theory of Party Organization," *Journal of Politics* 46 (May 1984): 369–400.

11. Clinton Rossiter, *Parties and Politics in America* (Ithaca, N.Y.: Cornell University Press, 1960), p. 37.

12. E. E. Schattschneider, *Party Government* (New York: Holt, Rinehart and Winston, 1942), pp. 131–32; italics in the original.

13. See Joseph Schlesinger, *Ambition in Politics* (Chicago: Rand-McNally, 1965).

14. James Madison, *The Federalist*, No. 51 (1788; New York: Modern Library, 1941), p. 337.

15. Richard Fenno, *Home Style* (Boston: Little Brown, 1978), pp. 127–28.

16. Julius Turner, "Responsible Parties: A Dissent from the Floor," *American Political Science Review* 45 (March 1951): 151.

17. John Kingdon, *Congressmen's Voting Decisions* (New York: Random House, 1968).

18. Milton Rakove, *Don't Make No Waves, Don't Back No Losers* (Bloomington: Indiana University Press, 1975), p. 164.

19. Leon Epstein, *Political Parties in the American Mold* (Madison: University of Wisconsin Press, 1986), pp. 129–32. On presidential nominations, see Howard Reiter, *Selecting the President* (Philadelphia: University of Pennsylvania Press, 1985), chaps. 1, 7.

20. William Brown, *The People's Choice* (Baton Rouge: Louisiana State University Press, 1960).

21. Richard Jensen, *The Winning of the Midwest* (Chicago: University of Chicago Press, 1971), p. 165.

22. Ibid.

23. David Mayhew, *Congress: The Electoral Connection* (New Haven, Conn.: Yale University Press, 1974); Morris Fiorina, *Congress: Keystone of the Washington Establishment* (New Haven, Conn.: Yale University Press, 1977).

24. Barbara Hinckley, *Congressional Elections* (Washington, D. C.: Congressional Quarterly Press, 1981), chap. 2.

25. Fenno, *Home Style*, p. 246.

26. Joseph Schlesinger, "The New American Political Party," *American Political Science Review* 79 (Dec. 1985): 1168.

27. Max Weber, "Politics as a Vocation," in *From Max Weber*, ed. H. H. Gerth and C. Wright Mills (New York: Galaxy, 1958), pp. 79–80.

28. Franz Neumann, *Behemoth* (1944; New York: Harper, 1966), esp. chap. 1, p. 3.

29. This phrase is attributed to Bentham by John Stuart Mill, in *Utilitarianism*, ed. Mary Warnock (1861; London: Collins, 1962), chap. 5, p. 319. No precise source has ever been located, but Bentham comes close to stating these words in his defense of universal suffrage. See "Plan of Parliamentary Reform," in *Works of Jeremy Bentham*, ed. John Browning, 7 vols. (1817; Edinburgh: Simkin, Marshall, 1843), vol. 3, sec. 7, pp. 459–65. I am grateful to Professor F. Rosen, University College, London, for locating this source.

30. Bentham, *Principles*, p. 3.

31. Mill, *Utilitarianism*, Book 2, p. 268.

32. Ibid., "Introduction," p. 28.

33. Downs, *Economic Theory*, pp. 267–68.

34. Ibid., p. 27.

35. See Robert Stubbings and Edward Carmines, "Is It Rational to Vote?" *Polity* 23 (Summer 1991): 629–40.

36. See Dennis Hale's insightful example, "Politics, Economics and Parking Spaces," *Teaching Political Science* 13 (Summer 1986): 154–59.

37. Alexis de Tocqueville, *Democracy in America*, ed. Phillips Bradley, 2 vols. (1835/1840; New York: Vintage, 1954), 1: 243.

38. Walter Lippmann, *The Public Philosophy* (New York: New American Library, 1955), pp. 23–24.

39. Benjamin Page and Robert Shapiro, "Changes in Americans' Policy Preferences, 1935–1979," *Public Opinion Quarterly* 46 (Spring 1982): 24–42; Benjamin Page and Robert Shapiro, *The Rational Public* (Chicago: University of Chicago Press, 1992).

40. Denise L. Baer and David A. Bositis, *Elite Cadres and Party Coalitions: Representing the Public in Party Politics* (New York: Greenwood Press, 1988), p. 39.

41. Weber, "Politics as a Vocation," p. 128.

CHAPTER SEVEN: PARTY CONCEPTS AND VOTING BEHAVIOR

1. W. L. Riordan, *Plunkitt of Tammany Hall* (New York: E. P. Dutton, 1963), p.6.

2. Joseph Schumpeter, *Capitalism, Socialism, and Democracy* (New York: Harper, 1950), pp. 269, 285.

3. This tripartite explanation obviously stems from the classic study of electoral behavior: Angus Campbell, Philip Converse, Warren Miller, and Donald Stokes, *The American Voter* (New York: Wiley, 1960).

4. Gerald Pomper, *The Election of 1988* (Chatham, N.J.: Chatham House, 1989), p. 142.

5. *Congressional Quarterly Weekly Report* 38 (Nov. 1, 1980): pp. 3288–89.

6. Arthur Miller and Martin Wattenberg, "Throwing the Rascals Out: Policy and Performance Evaluations of Presidential Candidates, 1952–1980," *American Political Science Review* 79 (June 1985): 359–72.

7. M. Ostrogorski, *Democracy and the Organization of Political Parties*, ed. Seymour Lipset, 2 vols. (1902; New York: Doubleday Anchor, 1964), 2:29–30.

8. Noble Cunningham, "Election of 1800," in *The Coming to Power*, ed. Arthur Schlesinger, Jr. (New York: Chelsea House, 1971), pp. 33–66; the quotations are on pp. 50 and 33.

9. Richard Wright, *The God That Failed* (New York: Bantam, 1952), p. 119; cf. Maurice Duverger, *Political Parties* (London: Methuen, 1954), p. 119.

10. Lawrence Goodwyn, *The Populist Moment* (New York: Oxford University Press, 1978), pp. 178–79.

11. Riordan, *Plunkitt*, pp. 35–36. This ethical principle is exemplified in contemporary times by William Bulger, president of the Massachusetts state senate: See Richard Brookhiser, "Profiles: Dancing with the Girl That Brung Him," *The New Yorker*, Oct. 28, 1991, 44–84.

12. Frank Friedel, "Election of 1932," in *Coming to Power*, pp. 322–54; the quotations are on pp. 349 and 354.

13. Jody Carlson, *George C. Wallace and the Politics of Powerlessness* (New Brunswick, N.J.: Transaction Books, 1981), chap. 16.

14. G. Bingham Powell, Jr., "American Voter Turnout in Comparative Perspective," *American Political Science Review* 80 (March 1986): 17–44. The misleading aspects of the data are that other nations calculate turnout on a base of registered voters, not the total population. Moreover, because of multiple elections, Americans have more opportunities to vote: See Richard Boyd, "Decline of U.S. Voting Turnout: Structural Explanations," *American Politics Quarterly* 9 (April 1981): 133–59. Nevertheless, even with these corrections, U.S. participation is about the lowest in the democratic world (excluding Switzerland).

15. Stephen Bennett and David Resnick, "The Implications of Nonvoting for Democracy in the United States," *American Journal of Political Science* 34 (Aug. 1990): 776–82.

16. Raymond Wolfinger and Steven Rosenstone, *Who Votes?* (New Haven, Conn.: Yale University Press, 1980); Powell, "American Voter Turnout," pp. 33–35.

17. On the effect of parties within the United States today, see Gregory Caldeira, Samuel Patterson, and Gregory Markko, "The Mobilization of Voters in Congressional Elections," *Journal of Politics* 47 (May 1985): 490–505.

18. Merrill Shanks and Warren Miller develop these various factors in their detailed analysis of presidential elections in the 1980s. See Miller, "The Election of 1984 and the Future of American Politics," in *Elections in America*, ed. Kay Lehman Schlozman (Boston: Allen and Unwin, 1987), pp. 293–320; Shanks and Miller, "Alternative Interpretations of the 1988 Election" (American Political Science Association, Atlanta, 1989).

19. V. O. Key and Frank Munger, "Social Determinism and Electoral Decision," in *American Voting Behavior*, ed. Eugene Burdick and Arthur Brodbeck (New York: Free Press, 1959), pp. 281–99. See Warren Miller, "Party Identification, Realignment and Party Voting," *American Political Science Review* 85 (June 1991): 557–68.

20. Paul Lazarsfeld, Bernard Berelson, and Helen Gaudet, *The People's Choice*, 2d ed. (New York: Columbia University Press, 1948), p. 27.

21. M. Kent Jennings and Richard Niemi, *Generations and Politics* (Princeton, N.J.: Princeton University Press, 1981), pp. 48–54.

22. Harold Stanley, William Bianco, and Richard Niemi, "Partisanship and Group Support over Time," *American Political Science Review* 80 (Sept. 1986): 971; Harold Stanley and Richard Niemi, "Partisanship and Group Support, 1952–1988" (American Political Science Association, Atlanta, 1989), Tables 2–5.

23. Peggy Noonan, *What I Saw at the Revolution* (New York: Random House, 1990), p. 102.

24. Wilson Carey McWilliams, "Parties as Civic Associations," in *Party Renewal in America*, ed. Gerald Pomper (New York: Praeger, 1980), p. 63.

25. Charles H. Franklin and John E. Jackson, "The Dynamics of Party Identification," *American Political Science Review* 77 (Dec. 1983): 957–73.

26. Major writings in a large literature include V. O. Key, "A Theory of Critical Elections," *Journal of Politics* 17 (Feb. 1955): 3–18; Walter Dean Burnham, *Critical Elections and the Mainsprings of American Politics* (New York: Norton, 1970); James Sundquist, *Dynamics of the Party System*, rev. ed. (Washington, D.C.: Brookings, 1983); and Edward Carmines and James Stimson, *Issue Evolution* (Princeton, N.J.: Princeton University Press, 1989).

27. Martin Wattenberg, *The Decline of American Political Parties* (Cambridge, Mass.: Harvard University Press, 1984), pp. 50, 69.

28. Leon Epstein, *Political Parties in the American Mold* (Madison: University of Wisconsin Press, 1986), p. 262.

29. Morris Fiorina, *Retrospective Voting in American National Elections* (New Haven, Conn.: Yale University Press, 1981), p. 200.

30. Paul Abramson, John Aldrich, and David Rohde, *Change and Continuity in the 1988 Elections* (Washington, D. C.: Congressional Quarterly Press, 1990), p. 186.

31. Richard Brody and Benjamin Page, "Comment: The Assessment of Policy Voting," *American Political Science Review* 66 (June 1972): 450–58.

32. Philip Converse showed the absence of coherent voter ideologies in his classic work, "The Nature of Belief Systems in Mass Publics," in *Ideology and Discontent*, ed. David Apter (Glencoe, Ill.: The Free Press, 1964). Evidence of increased mass ideological understanding is presented in Norman Nie and Kristi Andersen, "Mass Belief Systems Revisited," *Journal of Politics* 36 (Aug. 1974): 540–91. Kathleen Knight explores the contemporary meaning of mass ideology in a number of important studies, e.g., "Ideology in the 1980 Election," *Journal of Politics* 47 (Aug. 1985): 828–53. See also Pamela Conover and Stanley Feldman, "The Origins and Meaning of Liberal/Conservative Self-Identification," *American Journal of Political Science* 25 (Nov. 1981): 607–45.

33. See, for example, Mark Peffley and Jon Hurwitz, "A Hierarchical Model of Attitude Constraint," *American Journal of Political Science* 29 (Nov. 1985): 871–90; Eric Smith, *The Unchanging American Voter* (Berkeley: University of California Press, 1989); Richard Lau and David Sears, eds., *Political Cognition* (Hillsdale, N.J.: Lawrence Erlbaum, 1986).

34. V. O. Key, *The Responsible Electorate* (Cambridge, Mass.: Harvard University Press, 1966), p. 8.

35. John E. Jackson, "Issues, Party Choices, and Presidential Votes," *American Journal of Political Science* 21 (Aug. 1977): 161–86. An excellent review of the scholarship on issue voting is found in Michael Gant and Norman Luttbeg, *American Electoral Behavior* (Itasca, Ill.: Peacock, 1991), chap. 2.

36. Fiorina, *Retrospective Voting*, p. 197.

37. George Rabinowitz and Stuart Elaine MacDonald, "A Directional Theory of Issue Voting," *American Political Science Review* 83 (March 1989): 93–121.

38. Jeffrey Smith, *American Presidential Elections* (New York: Praeger, 1980).

39. Arthur Miller, Martin Wattenberg, and Oksana Malanchuk, "Schematic Assessments of Presidential Candidates," *American Political Science Review* 80 (June 1986): 535–36.

40. Gant and Luttbeg develop this original analysis in *American Electoral Behavior*, pp. 67–72.

41. This is the common thread of several studies: Gerald Pomper, *Voters' Choice* (New York: Harper & Row, 1975); Sidney Verba, Norman Nie, and John Petrocik, *The Changing American Voter* (Cambridge, Mass.: Harvard University Press, 1976); Eugene DeClerq, Thomas Hurley, and Norman Luttbeg, "Voting in American Presidential Elections," *American Politics Quarterly* 3 (July 1975), updated in Gant and Luttbeg, *American Electoral Behavior*, p. 64. Sophisticated probit analyses underline changes in the relative impacts of the factors affecting voters (private communication by John Kessel). If the voting decision were a recipe, it would today include, roughly, three measures of issues to two of candidates to one of partisanship. In the 1950s, the blend was, respectively, two to one and a half to one.

42. The expectations of the governing caucus model fit the voting pattern on three of

the four factors, the only case of such high agreement. If we use a different standard, the office-seeking model is also close to the empirical evidence. This alternative standard is the arithmetic, algebraic difference between expectations and reality, with "low" scored 1, "moderate" 2, and "high" 3. In these calculations, the governing caucus model is only two total units from the empirical reality, and the office-seeking model three units. All other models show a greater difference.

43. See Ross Baker, *The New Fat Cats* (New York: Twentieth Century Fund, 1989); Larry Sabato, *The Party's Just Begun* (Glenview, Ill.: Scott, Foresman, 1988), chap. 3.

44. Judson James early suggested a similar concept of parties although with greater emphasis on party loyalty and the president. See his description of "national executive-centered coalitions" in *American Political Parties in Transition* (New York: Harper & Row, 1974), chap. 11.

CHAPTER EIGHT: THE REFORM OF POLITICAL PARTIES

1. James Madison, *The Federalist*, No. 10 (1787; New York: Modern Library, 1941), p. 56.

2. Austin Ranney, *Curing the Mischiefs of Faction* (Berkeley: University of California Press, 1975), pp. 20f.

3. The national primary was supported by 65 percent of a national sample in 1988; *The Gallup Poll: Public Opinion 1988* (Wilmington, Del.: Scholarly Resources, 1989), p. 60.

4. Nelson Polsby, *Consequences of Party Reform* (New York: Oxford University Press, 1983), p. 72.

5. Leon Epstein, *Political Parties in the American Mold* (Madison: University of Wisconsin Press, 1986), chap. 6.

6. Robert LaFollette, 1900, cited by Ranney, *Curing the Mischiefs*, p. 125.

7. M. Ostrogorski, *Democracy and the Organization of Political Parties*, ed. Seymour Martin Lipset, 2 vols. (1902; New York: Doubleday Anchor, 1964), 2: 356f.

8. Madison, *Federalist*, No. 10, p. 54.

9. Epstein, *Political Parties*, pp. 343–44.

10. *Rutan* v. *Republican Party of Illinois*, 111 L.Ed. 2d 52 (1990), at 66. The only academic citation on this point is to Larry Sabato, *Goodbye to Good-Time Charlie*, 2d ed. (Washington, D.C.: Congressional Quarterly Press, 1983). This fine work deals not with political parties but with the increasing powers and abilities of American state governors.

11. *Rutan*, at 66f. Relevant earlier decisions are *Elrod* v. *Burns*, 427 U.S. 347 (1976), and *Branti* v. *Finkel*, 445 U.S. 507 (1980).

12. *Rutan*, at 78.

13. Ibid., at 78–88.

14. Eugene Lee, *The Politics of Nonpartisanship* (Berkeley: University of California Press, 1960).

15. In New York State, ten thousand public officials are covered by this ban. See Howard Scarrow, "Political Parties and the Law" (American Political Science Association, San Francisco, 1990), pp. 9–11.

16. In 1964, Jack Dennis found 22 percent agreeing that, "It would be better if, in

all elections, we put no party labels on the ballot,'' while 67 percent disagreed; see "Support for the Party System by the Mass Public," *American Political Science Review* 60 (Sept. 1966); 600–15. By 1984, disagreement, the proparty position, had decreased to 45 percent; see Jack Dennis, "Public Support for the Party System, 1964–1984" (American Political Science Association, Washington, D.C., 1986), Table 2.

17. Charles Gilbert, "Some Aspects of Nonpartisan Elections in Large Cities," *Midwest Journal of Political Science* 6 (Nov. 1962): 345–62; Susan Welch and Timothy Bledsoe, "The Partisan Consequences of Nonpartisan Elections and the Changing Nature of Urban Politics," *American Journal of Political Science* 30 (Feb. 1986): 128–39.

18. Robert Lineberry and Edmund Fowler, "Reformism and Public Policies in American Cities," *American Political Science Review* 61 (Sept. 1967): 715.

19. Henry Jones Ford, "The Direct Primary," *North American Review* 190 (July 1909): 2–9. See also, H. J. Ford, "Municipal Corruption," a scathing review of Lincoln Steffens's classic, *The Shame of the Cities*, in *Political Science Quarterly* 19 (Dec. 1904): 679–81. I am indebted to Patrick Deneen for pointing out these two articles to me.

20. Lewis Chester, Godfrey Hodgson, and Bruce Page, *An American Melodrama* (New York: Viking, 1969), p. 231.

21. See Christopher Arterton, "Political Money and Party Strength," in *The Future of American Political Parties*, ed. Joel Fleishman (New York: American Assembly, 1982), chap. 4.

22. *Buckley* v. *Valeo*, 424 U.S. 1 (1976).

23. Ibid., at 19.

24. Committee on Political Parties, "Toward a More Responsible Two-Party System," *American Political Science Review* 44 (Sept. 1950): *Supplement*. An important later program along similar lines was Stephen Bailey's work, *The Condition of Our Political Parties* (New York: Fund for the Republic, 1959).

25. Denise L. Baer and David A. Bositis, *Elite Cadres and Party Coalitions* (Westport, Conn.: Greenwood, 1988), p. 172. These authors use the term "responsible parties" for what I have called the "party government" perspective, but our meanings are essentially the same.

26. Michael Oreskes, "Deficit Pact Blurs Party Boundaries," *New York Times*, Oct. 14, 1990, D22.

27. John White, "Responsible Party Government in America" (Northeastern Political Science Association, Providence, R.I., 1990), p. 20.

28. Evron Kirkpatrick, "Toward a More Responsible Two-Party System: Political Science, Policy Science, or Pseudo-Science?" *American Political Science Review* 65 (Dec. 1971): 965–90; Leon Epstein, "What Happened to the British Party Model?" *American Political Science Review* 74 (March 1980): 9–22.

29. See Charles Hardin, *Presidential Power and Accountability* (Chicago: University of Chicago Press, 1974), chap. 10, and Donald Robinson, *Government for the Third American Century* (Boulder, Colo.: Westview, 1989), chaps. 7–9. On constitutional reform more generally, see the Bicentennial Papers of the Committee on the Constitutional System, in *Reforming American Government*, ed. Donald Robinson (Boulder, Colo.: Westview, 1985).

30. Committee on Political Parties, "Toward a More Responsible Two-Party System," passim.

31. Hanna Pitkin, *The Concept of Representation* (Berkeley: University of California Press, 1967), esp. chaps. 4, 6, 7, 10.

32. The problems are evident from the American Political Science Association (APSA) report to the McGovern-Fraser report, *Mandate for Reform* (Washington, D.C.: Democratic National Committee, 1970).

33. Ranney, *Curing the Mischiefs*, p. 114.

34. Polsby, *Consequences*, p. 152.

35. *Nixon* v. *Condon*, 76 L.Ed. 984 (1931), Justice Cardozo's majority opinion, at 990.

36. *Grovey* v. *Townsend*, 70 L.Ed. 1292 (1934), Justice Roberts's majority opinion, at 1296.

37. *Smith* v. *Allwright*, 88 L.Ed. 987 (1943), Justice Reed's majority opinion at 997. The final burial of the "white primary" came in *Terry* v. *Adams*, 345 U.S. 461 (1953).

38. John Kester, "Constitutional Restrictions on Political Parties," *Virginia Law Review* 60 (May 1974): 756–77.

39. *Brown* v. *O'Brien*, 409 U.S. 1, 816 (1972); *Cousins* v. *Wigoda*, 419 U.S. 477 (1975); *Democratic Party* v. *Wisconsin ex rel. LaFollette*, 450 U.S. 107 (1981); *Tashjian* v. *Republican party of Connecticut*, 479 U.S. 208 (1986).

40. *Eu* v. *San Francisco County Democratic Central Committee*, 109 S. Ct. 1013 (1989), at 1, 15.

41. Cornelius Cotter and John Bibby, "Institutional Development of Parties and the Thesis of Party Decline," *Political Science Quarterly* 95 (Spring 1980): 1–27.

42. See John Hart, "The End of Party Reform," in *Studies in US Politics*, ed. David Adams (Manchester, England: Manchester University Press, 1989), chap. 7.

43. Center for Responsive Politics, *Soft Money—A Loophole for the '80s* (Washington, D.C.: Commission on National Elections, 1985).

44. *Commission on National Elections, Electing the President: A Program for Reform* (Washington, D.C.: Georgetown University Center for Strategic and International Studies, 1986).

45. Howard Reiter, *Selecting the President* (Philadelphia: University of Pennsylvania Press, 1985), chap. 1.

46. The position is most strongly argued by Polsby, *Consequences*, and James Ceasar, *Reforming the Reforms* (Cambridge, Mass.: Bellinger, 1982).

47. See Baer and Bositis, *Elite Cadres*; David Price, *Bringing Back the Parties* (Washington, D.C.: Congressional Quarterly Press, 1984); Larry Sabato, *The Party's Just Begun* (Glenview, Ill.: Scott, Foresman, 1988).

48. Wilson Carey McWilliams, "The Anti-Federalists, Representation, and Party," *Northwestern University Law Review* 84 (Fall 1989): 28, 36.

49. E. E. Schattschneider, *Party Government* (New York: Holt, Rinehart and Winston, 1942), p. 60. This is of course the dilemma originally stated by Michels. See William Wright's classification of parties as "rational-efficient" or as examples of "party democracy" in *A Comparative Study of Party Organization* (Columbus, Ohio: Charles E. Merrill, 1971), pp. 17–54.

50. Walt Whitman, "Song of Myself," in *Leaves of Grass* (1855; New York: Modern Library, 1950), p. 74.

CHAPTER NINE: COMMON IMPULSES

1. Henry St. John Bolingbroke, *The Idea of a Patriot King*, ed. Sydney Jackman (1749; Indianapolis: Bobbs-Merrill, 1965), p. 47.

2. M. Ostrogorski, *Democracy and the Organization of Political Parties*, ed. Seymour Martin Lipset, 2 vols. (1902; New York: Doubleday Anchor, 1964), 2: 326.

3. Jack Dennis, "Support for the Party System by the Mass Public," *American Political Science Review* 60 (Sept. 1966): 605 and "Trends in Public Support for the American Party System," *British Journal of Political Science* 5 (April 1975): 200–8.

4. Hans Daadler, "The Comparative Study of European Parties and Party Systems: An Overview," in *West European Party Systems*, ed. Hans Daadler and Peter Mair (Beverly Hills, Calif.: Sage Publications, 1983), pp. 3–4.

5. Benito Mussolini, "The Political and Social Doctrine of Fascism," in *Social and Political Philosophy*, ed. John Somerville and Ronald Santoni (Garden City, N.Y.: Anchor Books, 1963), p. 437.

6. Jean Jacques Rousseau, *The Social Contract*, trans. G. D. H. Cole (1762; New York: Dutton, 1950), p. 23.

7. Ibid., p. 94. In modern times, the democratist view is well presented by Benjamin Barber, "The Undemocratic Party System," in *Political Parties in the Eighties*, ed. Robert Goldwin (Washington, D.C.: American Enterprise Institute, 1980), chap. 3.

8. James Madison, *The Federalist*, No. 10 (1787; New York: Modern Library, 1941), p. 53.

9. James Richardson, ed., *Messages and Papers of the Presidents* (Washington, D.C.: Government Printing Office, 1897), pp. 209-11.

10. *Inaugural Addresses of the Presidents of the United States* (Washington, D.C.: Government Printing Office, 1989), pp. 305, 349.

11. Richard Hofstadter, *The Idea of a Party System* (Berkeley: University of California Press, 1970), p. 151; James McG. Burns, *Roosevelt: The Lion and the Fox* (New York: Harcourt Brace, 1956), pp. 466–67; Sherman Adams, *Firsthand Report* (New York: Harper, 1961).

12. James Lord Bryce, Preface to Ostrogorski, *Democracy*, p. lxxiv–v.

13. H. J. Ford, "Municipal Corruption," *Political Science Quarterly* 19 (Dec. 1904): 679–80.

14. Ostrogorski, *Democracy*, p. 324.

15. William Kornhauser, *The Politics of Mass Society* (New York: Free Press, 1959), p. 60.

16. Mason made the remark in the Constitutional Convention's July 17 debate on the election of the president, James Madison, *Notes of Debates in the Federal Convention of 1787* (Athens: Ohio University Press, 1966), p. 308.

17. John Stuart Mill, *Considerations on Representative Government* (1862; New York: Liberal Arts Press, 1958), p. 131.

18. Mancur Olson, *The Logic of Collective Action* (Cambridge, Mass.: Harvard University Press, 1965).

19. Kornhauser, *Politics of Mass Society*, pp. 230–31.

20. Alexis de Tocqueville, *Democracy in America*, ed. Phillips Bradley, 2 vols. (1835/1840; New York: Vintage, 1954), 2: 109–10.

21. Robert Dahl, *After the Revolution?* (New Haven, Conn.: Yale University Press, 1970), chap. 1.

22. James Lord Bryce, "Why Great Men Are Not Chosen Presidents," *The American Commonwealth*, 2 vols. (London: Macmillan, 1889), vol. 1, chap. 8; Nelson Polsby, *Consequences of Party Reform* (New York: Oxford University Press, 1983), chap. 3; Stephen Hess, "'Why Great Men Are Not Chosen Presidents': Lord Bryce

Revisited," in *Elections American Style*, ed. James Reichley (Washington, D.C.: Brookings, 1987), chap. 4.

23. Alan Ware, *Citizens, Parties and the State* (Princeton, N.J.: Princeton University Press, 1987), chap. 1.

24. John Locke, *Of Civil Government*, Book 2, chap. 13 (1690; London: Everyman, 1924), p. 192.

25. Mill, *Representative Government*, p. 40.

26. Raymond Aron, quoted by Donald Robinson, "The Place of Party in Democratic Ideas," in *Party Renewal in America*, ed. Gerald Pomper (New York: Praeger, 1981), p. 22.

27. Tocqueville, *Democracy in America*, 1: 330.

28. Jane Mansbridge, *Beyond Adversary Democracy* (Chicago: University of Chicago Press, 1980).

29. Madison, *Federalist*, No. 51, p. 337.

30. Ibid., No. 10, pp. 58–59.

31. Rousseau, *Social Contract*, pp. 106, 93.

32. Alan Monroe, "American Party Platforms and Public Opinion," *American Journal of Political Science* 27 (Feb. 1983): 27–42; Benjamin Page and Robert Shapiro, "Effects of Public Opinion on Policy," *American Political Science Review* 77 (March 1983): 175–90.

33. Joseph Schumpeter, *Capitalism, Socialism, and Democracy* (New York: Harper, 1950), pp. 283–85.

34. Tocqueville, *Democracy in America*, 2: 124–25.

35. Note the critique of Anthony King and Giles Alston, "Good Government and the Politics of High Exposure," in Colin Campbell and Bert Rockman, *The Bush Presidency: First Appraisals* (Chatham, N.J.: Chatham House, 1991), chap. 9.

36. Alexander Hamilton, *The Federalist*, No. 70, p. 459.

37. Sidney Blumenthal, *The Perpetual Campaign*, rev. ed. (New York: Simon and Schuster, 1982), pp. 23–25.

38. Samuel Huntington, *American Politics: The Promise of Disharmony* (Cambridge, Mass.: Harvard University Press, 1981), p. 219.

39. These ideas draw on the program of the Committee for Party Renewal, reproduced in Robert Harmel and Kenneth Janda, *Parties and Their Environments* (New York: Longman, 1982), pp. 169–71. Another parallel reform plan can be found in Larry Sabato, *The Party's Just Begun* (Glenview, Ill.: Scott, Foresman, 1988), chaps. 6, 7.

40. Robert Michels, *Political Parties*, ed. Seymour Martin Lipset (1915; New York: Collier Books, 1962), p. 368.

INDEX